KRAFT®

make it SIMPLE

Recipe Collection

With today's fast-paced life, connecting with family and friends can be quite a challenge. Now with the help of the imaginative food ideas in *Kraft Make It Simple Recipe Collection,* you can carve out time for nurturing and nourishing, and turn mealtime into sharing time. Made with convenient family-pleasing products from Kraft and tested in the Kraft Kitchens, every recipe combines ease, style and great taste to bring irresistible dishes to your table. Plus, you'll find this book is full of hints for keeping kitchen time to a minimum.

Celebrate life's simple pleasures by trying these easy-on-the-cook recipes. You can be assured of delicious and successful results time after time.

CONTENTS

© Kraft Foods, Inc. and Meredith Corporation, 1999.
All rights reserved.
Produced by Meredith® Books,
1716 Locust St., Des Moines, IA 50309-3023.
ISBN: 0-696-20972-1 Printed in the United States of America.

Shown on front cover: PHILADELPHIA® Cream Cheese Classic
Cheesecake (recipe, page 200)

Marinated Olives
(recipe, page 7)

Meze Platter
(recipe, page 6)

Spicy Spanish Walnuts
(recipe, page 6)

EVERYDAY APPETIZERS & SNACKS

Whether the party's planned or spur-of-the moment, there's no better way to welcome guests to your home than with this irresistible assortment of appetizers and snacks. Choose from recipes such as Simple Smokie Squares, Italian Spinach Dip or Nacho Platter Olé and you'll have the fixings for a fun-filled get-together on the table in practically no time.

Spicy Spanish Walnuts

(Photo on pages 4–5.)

Prep time: 10 minutes   Baking time: 20 minutes

Makes 2 cups

2 tablespoons butter *or* margarine	**Melt** butter in medium saucepan on low heat. Add sugar, peels and spices.
3 tablespoons sugar	
2 teaspoons *each* grated orange peel and lime peel	**Toss** walnuts with spice mixture. Spoon onto cookie sheet.
1 teaspoon *each* ground coriander, ground cinnamon and ground cloves	
¼ teaspoon *each* ground red pepper and salt	**Bake** at 300°F for 20 minutes or until walnuts are toasted, stirring every 5 minutes. Cool.
2 cups walnut halves	

Meze Platter

(Photo on pages 4–5.)

Prep time: 20 to 30 minutes for grilling vegetables

Assorted grilled vegetables (such as zucchini pieces, roasted red pepper strips, thinly sliced potatoes and eggplant pieces) (tip, page 133)	**Arrange** vegetables, spreads, olives and pita triangles on large serving platter. Garnish with fresh herbs.
Assorted ATHENOS Mediterranean Spreads (Hummus, 3-Pepper Hummus, Whipped Feta Spread and Whipped Feta Spread with Tomato & Basil)	
Marinated Olives (recipe opposite page)	
Pita bread, cut into triangles	

Marinated Olives
(Photo on pages 4–5.)

Prep time: 5 minutes plus refrigerating
Makes 1¾ cups

1 can (6 ounces) pitted ripe olives, drained
    Greek, Italian, Spanish *or* French Seasonings (see right)

Mix olives and seasonings. Refrigerate 2 hours or overnight. Stir in chunks of fresh mozzarella, if desired.

Seasonings

Greek: 2 tablespoons olive oil, 1 tablespoon *each* fresh lemon juice and red wine vinegar and 1 teaspoon dried oregano leaves.

Italian: 2 tablespoons olive oil, 1 clove garlic, minced, ½ teaspoon dried basil leaves and ¼ teaspoon crushed red pepper.

Spanish: 2 tablespoons olive oil, 1 tablespoon red wine vinegar, 1 clove garlic, minced, 2 teaspoons finely chopped chives and ¼ teaspoon *each* ground red pepper and paprika.

French: 2 tablespoons olive oil and 2 cloves garlic, minced.

Grilled *Italian* Focaccia

Prep time: 10 minutes plus rising   Grilling time: 8 minutes

Makes 2 bread rounds or 16 servings

1   **package (16 ounces) hot roll mix**
1   **envelope GOOD SEASONS Italian Salad Dressing Mix**
3   **tablespoons olive oil, divided**
1   **cup DI GIORNO Shredded Parmesan Cheese**
2   **plum tomatoes, sliced**
2   **tablespoons fresh basil leaves**

Mix hot roll mix, yeast packet and salad dressing mix. Add 1¼ cups hot water (120°F to 130°F) and 2 tablespoons of the oil. Stir until soft dough forms and dough pulls away from side of bowl.

Knead dough on lightly floured surface about 5 minutes or until smooth and elastic. Shape dough into 2 (10-inch) rounds. Cover with plastic wrap or towel. Let rise in warm place 15 minutes.

Place dough rounds on greased grill over medium-low coals. Grill 4 minutes; turn. Brush with remaining 1 tablespoon oil. Top with cheese, tomatoes and basil. Grill an additional 4 minutes or until bottom crust is golden brown.

Crispy Chicken with *Honey Dipping* Sauce

Prep time: 10 minutes   Baking time: 14 minutes

Makes 8 servings

1   cup KRAFT Mayo: Real *or* Light Mayonnaise
¼   cup honey
2   tablespoons Dijon mustard *or* Chinese hot mustard
2   tablespoons peanut butter
4   boneless skinless chicken breast halves (about 1¼ pounds), cut into strips
1½ cups finely crushed potato chips

Mix mayo, honey, mustard and peanut butter. Remove ½ cup of the mayo mixture; set remaining aside.

Brush chicken with ½ cup of the mayo mixture; coat with crushed chips. Place on greased cookie sheet.

Bake at 425°F for 7 to 9 minutes. Turn. Bake an additional 4 to 5 minutes or until lightly browned. Serve with remaining mayo mixture as dipping sauce. Garnish with fresh chives.

Simple *Smokie* Squares

Prep time: 10 minutes   Baking time: 12 minutes

Makes about 4 dozen

2   cans (10 ounces *each*) refrigerated pizza crust
1   package (16 ounces) OSCAR MAYER Little Smokies *or* Little Wieners
1   package (8 ounces) KRAFT Shredded Colby/Monterey Jack Cheese

Spray 2 cookie sheets with no stick cooking spray. Unroll each pizza crust onto 1 cookie sheet.

Arrange Little Smokies evenly on each crust; press lightly into crust. Sprinkle each crust with 1 cup of cheese.

Bake at 425°F for 12 minutes or until golden brown. Cut into squares.

Hummus & *Vegetable* Pita Toasts

Prep time: 10 minutes

Pita bread, split
Olive oil
ATHENOS Mediterranean Spreads
  (Hummus and 3-Pepper Hummus)
Sliced green onions and shredded
  carrots
Sliced ripe olives

Brush cut side of pita bread rounds with oil. Place on cookie sheet. Broil 1 minute or until crisp.

Spread each pita bread round with 2 tablespoons hummus.

Sprinkle with vegetables. Cut each round into 4 wedges to serve.

Note: Hummus is one of the most widely known dishes of the Middle East. The distinctive spread of mashed garbanzo beans takes a prominent place on appetizer tables on this side of the Atlantic, too.

Rely on KRAFT Dips

A word to the wise—keep KRAFT Dips on hand for quick snacks. Serve with breadsticks, chips, crackers and vegetable dippers. Also, don't limit KRAFT Dips to just snacks. To add zip to your dinner, try KRAFT Dips on baked potatoes to liven up their flavor.

Black Bean and Mango Salsa

Prep time: 10 minutes plus refrigerating

Makes about 5 cups

1   **envelope GOOD SEASONS Italian Salad Dressing Mix**
1   **can (16 ounces) black beans, drained, rinsed**
1   **package (10 ounces) frozen corn, thawed**
1   **cup chopped ripe mango**
½   **cup chopped red pepper**
⅓   **cup *each* chopped cilantro and chopped red onion**
¼   **cup lime juice**

Mix all ingredients in large bowl. Refrigerate.

Serve with pita bread wedges, tortilla chips or grilled chicken. Serve in pepper halves, if desired.

Black Bean & Mango Salsa Salad: Prepare recipe as directed. Add 1½ cups cooked brown rice.

Colorful Containers

For a splash of color, serve dips and spreads in edible containers—hollowed-out round bread loaves, bell peppers, zucchini and small red or green cabbages are great to make into "bowls." After filling it with your dip, set the "bowl" on a serving plate and surround it with an assortment of crackers, chips or bite-size veggies.

Fruit & Cheese Bites

Prep time: 10 minutes

Makes 20

20 table wafer crackers *or any cracker*
 1 package (10 ounces) CRACKER BARREL
    Extra Sharp Natural Cheddar Cheese,
    sliced
    Strawberry slices
    Kiwi slices, cut into eighths
 ¼ cup orange marmalade

Top crackers with cheese slices, fruit and marmalade. Garnish with fresh mint leaves.

Pickle Bunny *Bites*

Prep time: 15 minutes plus marinating

Makes about 32

1 envelope GOOD SEASONS Zesty Herb Salad Dressing Mix for Fat Free Dressing

16 baby carrots, cut in half lengthwise

1 package (6 ounces) OSCAR MAYER Boiled Ham, cut into 4 strips

1 jar (20 ounces) CLAUSSEN Mini Kosher Dill Pickles, drained, cut in half lengthwise

Prepare salad dressing mix as directed on package. Place salad dressing and carrot halves in zipper-style plastic bag. Refrigerate 2 hours or overnight to marinate. Drain; reserve salad dressing.

Wrap 1 ham strip around 1 pickle half and 1 carrot half; secure with toothpick.

Serve with reserved salad dressing for dipping.

Turkey with Sesame Peanut Sauce (recipe below) and Smokie Wraps with Honey Dijon Dipping Sauce (recipe, page 21)

Turkey with *Sesame Peanut* Sauce

Prep time: 10 minutes

Makes 40

1	**pound LOUIS RICH Breast of Turkey**
¾	**cup orange marmalade**
¼	**cup peanut butter**
3	**tablespoons teriyaki sauce**
2	**teaspoons toasted sesame seeds**

Cut turkey into bite-size cubes; spear cubes with toothpicks. Garnish with pepper cutouts.

Mix remaining ingredients in small bowl. Stir until well blended. Garnish with green onion strips. Serve sauce as dip for turkey.

18

SHAKE 'N BAKE® *Chicken Nuggets*

Prep time: 10 minutes   Baking time: 15 minutes

Makes 4 to 6 servings

5   **boneless skinless chicken breast halves**
1   **packet SHAKE 'N BAKE Seasoned Coating Mix for Chicken, Hot & Spicy *or* Classic Italian**

Cut chicken into 1½- to 2-inch pieces.

Shake chicken pieces with coating mix; discard any remaining mix.

Bake at 400°F for 10 to 15 minutes or until cooked through. Serve with KRAFT Sweet 'N Sour Sauce in a green pepper half, if desired.

Italian Spinach Dip

Prep time: 10 minutes plus refrigerating

Makes 3 cups

1   cup KRAFT Mayo Real Mayonnaise
1   cup BREAKSTONE'S *or* KNUDSEN
    Sour Cream
1   envelope GOOD SEASONS Italian Salad
    Dressing Mix
1   package (10 ounces) frozen chopped
    spinach, thawed, well drained
½   cup chopped red pepper (optional)

Mix mayo, sour cream and salad dressing mix until well blended. Add spinach and red pepper; mix well. Refrigerate.

Serve in hollowed-out red cabbage with assorted fresh vegetables.

Smokie Wraps with *Honey Dijon* Dipping Sauce

(Photo on page 18.)

Prep time: 10 minutes   Baking time: 8 minutes

Makes about 4 dozen

⅔   cup Dijon mustard
⅓   cup honey
10 flour tortillas (6-inch)
1   package (16 ounces) OSCAR MAYER Little
    Smokies *or* Little Wieners

Mix mustard and honey in small bowl.

Spread each tortilla lightly with mustard sauce. Cut each tortilla into 6 strips. Roll 1 Little Smokie in each strip; secure with toothpicks and place on nonstick cookie sheet (or sheet sprayed with no stick cooking spray). Reserve extra sauce for dipping.

Bake at 350°F for 5 to 8 minutes or until hot. Serve with reserved dipping sauce.

Creamy Italian Dip

Prep time: 10 minutes plus refrigerating

Makes 2 cups

1   cup **MIRACLE WHIP** *or* **MIRACLE WHIP LIGHT**
     Dressing

½   cup **BREAKSTONE'S** *or* **KNUDSEN Sour**
     Cream

1   envelope **GOOD SEASONS Italian, Zesty**
     Italian *or* **Garlic & Herb Salad**
     Dressing Mix

½   cup **finely chopped green pepper**

Mix all ingredients. Refrigerate. Garnish with summer savory and pineapple sage flower. Serve with assorted cut-up vegetables or crackers.

Hot *Artichoke Dip*

Prep time: 10 minutes   Baking time: 25 minutes

Makes 2 cups

1 **can (14 ounces) artichoke hearts, drained, chopped**
1 **cup (4 ounces) KRAFT 100% Grated Parmesan Cheese**
1 **cup KRAFT Mayo Real Mayonnaise *or* MIRACLE WHIP Salad Dressing**
1 **clove garlic, minced**
  Chopped tomato
  Sliced green onions

Mix all ingredients except tomato and onions.

Spoon into 9-inch pie plate or quiche dish.

Bake at 350°F for 20 to 25 minutes or until lightly browned. Sprinkle with tomato and onions. Garnish with flowering chive and strips of green onion. Serve with crackers.

Nacho Platter *Olé*

Prep time: 10 minutes   Microwave time: 10 minutes

Makes 6 to 8 servings

1 can (16 ounces) TACO BELL
   HOME ORIGINALS Refried Beans
1 package (8 to 11 ounces) tortilla chips
1 can (15 ounces) chili
1 jar (16 ounces) CHEEZ WHIZ Pasteurized
   Process Cheese Sauce

Spread beans onto center of large serving platter.

Arrange chips around beans. Heat chili as directed on label; pour over beans.

Microwave process cheese sauce as directed on label; pour over chili and chips. Garnish with shredded lettuce and chopped red pepper. Serve immediately.

TACO BELL and HOME ORIGINALS are registered trademarks owned and licensed by Taco Bell Corp.

Drop-In Guests

Keep on hand the few ingredients needed for Nacho Platter Olé, and within minutes, you can serve guests your delicious creation. For an extra-special presentation, make a footed platter by turning a saucer or small bowl upside down and placing the platter of nachos on top. Then, set the table with bowls of sour cream, salsa, chopped green onions, guacamole and tomatoes so guests can add more toppings to the nachos.

PHILADELPHIA® *Creamy Salsa* Dip

Prep time: 10 minutes plus refrigerating

Makes 2 cups

1 **package (8 ounces) PHILADELPHIA Cream Cheese, softened**

1 **cup TACO BELL HOME ORIGINALS Salsa, any variety**

Mix cream cheese and salsa until well blended. Refrigerate. Garnish with zucchini-and-carrot curl. Serve with crackers, tortilla chips or assorted cut-up vegetables.

Note: To make baked tortilla chips, cut flour tortillas into desired shapes. Place, in single layer, on cookie sheet. Bake at 350°F for 5 to 10 minutes or until dry and crisp. Remove from cookie sheet. Cool on wire rack.

TACO BELL and HOME ORIGINALS are registered trademarks owned and licensed by Taco Bell Corp.

VELVEETA® *Salsa* Dip

Prep time: 5 minutes   Microwave time: 5 minutes

Makes 3 cups

1   **pound (16 ounces) VELVEETA Pasteurized Process Cheese Spread, cut up**
1   **cup TACO BELL HOME ORIGINALS Thick 'N Chunky Salsa**

Microwave process cheese spread and salsa in 1½-quart microwavable bowl on HIGH 5 minutes or until process cheese spread is melted, stirring after 3 minutes. Serve hot with assorted tortilla chips or cut-up vegetables.

TACO BELL and HOME ORIGINALS are registered trademarks owned and licensed by Taco Bell Corp.

Hot Bacon Cheese Spread

Prep time: 15 minutes   Baking time: 1 hour

Makes 3½ cups

1   **loaf (16 ounces) round bread**
12   **slices OSCAR MAYER Center Cut Bacon,
     crisply cooked, crumbled**
1   **package (8 ounces) KRAFT Shredded
     Colby/Monterey Jack Cheese**
1   **cup (4 ounces) KRAFT 100% Grated
     Parmesan Cheese**
1   **cup KRAFT Mayo Real Mayonnaise**
1   **small onion, finely chopped**
1   **clove garlic, minced**

Cut lengthwise slice from top of bread loaf, remove center, leaving 1-inch-thick shell. Cut removed bread into bite-size pieces; set aside.

Mix remaining ingredients in small bowl. Spoon into hollowed bread shell. Cover shell with top of bread; place on cookie sheet.

Bake at 350°F for 1 hour. Serve with bread pieces or crackers.

Note: To reheat, microwave filled bread shell with top on HIGH 1 to 2 minutes or until thoroughly heated, stirring once.

Yogurt Dip

Prep time: 10 minutes plus refrigerating

Makes 1 cup

2   tablespoons KOOL-AID Sugar-Sweetened
    Soft Drink Mix, any flavor
1   container (8 ounces) BREYERS *or*
    KNUDSEN Vanilla Lowfat Yogurt *or*
    BREAKSTONE'S *or* KNUDSEN Sour Cream
    Cut-up fresh fruit

Stir soft drink mix into yogurt in medium bowl.

Refrigerate 1 hour or until ready to serve. Stir. Garnish with sliced strawberry and kiwi. Serve with fruit.

Candy Corn *Popcorn* Balls

Prep time: 15 minutes   Microwave time: 2 minutes

Makes 15

¼ **cup (½ stick) butter *or* margarine**
1 **package (10½ ounces) miniature marshmallows (6 cups)**
1 **package (4-serving size) JELL-O Gelatin Dessert, any flavor**
12 **cups (3 quarts) popped popcorn**
1 **cup candy corn**

Microwave butter and marshmallows in large microwavable bowl on HIGH 1½ to 2 minutes or until marshmallows are puffed. Stir in gelatin until well mixed.

Pour marshmallow mixture over popcorn and candy corn in large bowl. Mix lightly until well coated. Shape into 15 balls or other shapes with greased or wet hands. Wrap each ball in plastic wrap and tie with raffia or ribbon, if desired.

Popcorn Fix-Up

Popcorn is always a hit. To give it extra pizzazz, try this tasty variation. Place buttered popcorn in a paper lunch bag. Sprinkle with KRAFT 100% Grated Parmesan Cheese and GOOD SEASONS Italian Salad Dressing Mix. Shake until coated.

ABC Snack Mix

Prep time: 5 minutes

Makes about 10 cups

4   cups POST ALPHA-BITS Frosted Letter Oat
    and Corn Cereal, any variety
3   cups assorted festive candies
2   cups caramel popcorn
1   cup peanuts
1   cup small pretzels

Mix all ingredients in large bowl. Store in tightly covered container.

Simple Snack Mix

Be prepared when appetites won't wait. Keep ABC Snack Mix in easy-to-reach containers. Or, for other mixes, start with your favorite POST Sweetened Cereal and stir in tiny pretzels, miniature marshmallows, BAKER'S Semi-Sweet Chocolate Chips, popcorn, caramel popcorn, mixed nuts, raisins and/or other dried fruits.

OREO O's™ *Bars*

Prep time: 5 minutes plus cooling   Microwave time: 3 minutes

Makes 18

¼   **cup (½ stick) butter *or* margarine**
1   **package (10½ ounces) miniature marshmallows (6 cups)**
8   **cups POST OREO O's Cereal**

Microwave butter in 4-quart microwavable bowl on HIGH 45 seconds or until melted. Add marshmallows; mix to coat. Microwave 1½ minutes or until marshmallows are melted and smooth, stirring after 45 seconds. Add cereal; mix to coat well.

Press firmly into greased foil-lined 13×9-inch pan. Cool; cut into rectangles.

Chocolate OREO O's™ Bars: Prepare as directed, melting 2 squares BAKER'S Semi-Sweet Baking Chocolate with butter.

OREO O's is a trademark of Nabisco Brands Co. Used under license.

Design a Fruit Pizza

Cure your kids' between-meal hunger pangs with this quick-to-fix snack. Spread PHILADELPHIA FLAVORS Cheesecake Flavor Cream Cheese Spread onto a baked pizza crust or toasted English muffin. Top with sliced fresh fruit. Sprinkle with toasted coconut.

Marshmallow Crispy Treats

Prep time: 10 minutes   Microwave time: 2¼ minutes

Makes 2 dozen

¼ **cup (½ stick) butter *or* margarine**
1 **package (10½ ounces) miniature marshmallows (6 cups)**
1 **package (13 ounces) POST Fruity PEBBLES Cereal (about 8½ cups)**

Microwave butter in 4-quart microwavable bowl on HIGH 45 seconds or until melted. Add marshmallows; mix to coat. Microwave 1½ minutes or until marshmallows are melted and smooth; stir after 45 seconds. Add cereal; mix to coat well.

Press firmly into greased foil-lined 13×9-inch pan. Cool; cut into squares.

Coffee *Smoothie*

Prep time: 10 minutes

Makes 3 servings

1 cup chilled brewed double strength
   MAXWELL HOUSE Coffee, any variety
1 banana
1 container (8 ounces) vanilla lowfat
   yogurt
2 teaspoons sugar
¼ cup ice cubes

Place coffee, banana, yogurt, sugar and
ice cubes in blender container; cover.
Blend on high speed until smooth.
Serve immediately.

Sparkling *Raspberry Cranberry* Punch

Prep time: 10 minutes plus refrigerating

Makes 32 servings

1   tub CRYSTAL LIGHT Raspberry Ice Flavor
    Low Calorie Soft Drink Mix
1   tub CRYSTAL LIGHT Cranberry Breeze
    Flavor Low Calorie Soft Drink Mix
8   cups (2 quarts) cold water
2   bottles (1 liter *each*) chilled raspberry-
    flavored seltzer *or* seltzer
1   package (10 ounces) frozen
    raspberries, thawed
    Raspberry sorbet

Place drink mixes in punch bowl. Add water; stir to dissolve. Cover. Refrigerate.

Stir in seltzer and raspberries just before serving. Garnish with frozen ice ring and fresh cranberries. Serve with small scoops of sorbet.

Caramel Coffee

Prep time: 10 minutes

Makes 6 servings

6   **tablespoons MAXWELL HOUSE Coffee, any variety**
½   **cup KRAFT Caramel Dessert Topping**
4½ **cups cold water**

Place coffee in filter in brew basket of coffeemaker. Place topping in empty pot of coffeemaker. Prepare coffee with cold water. When brewing is complete, stir until well mixed. Top each serving with thawed COOL WHIP Whipped Topping and chopped chocolate-covered toffee, if desired.

15 Minute Chicken
& Rice Dinner
(recipe, page 42)

SHORTCUT FAMILY MEALS

The clock's ticking and the whole family's in a hurry, but enjoying a meal together is no problem. You can feed your family in just minutes with these simple and delicious recipes that are made with tasty, work-saving ingredients. Choose from dishes such as Oven BBQ Chicken, Quick Taco Quesadillas and Italian Pork Chops Mozzarella.

15 Minute Chicken & Rice Dinner

(Photo on pages 40–41.)

Prep/Cook time: 15 minutes

Makes 4 servings

1   **tablespoon oil***
4   **small boneless skinless chicken breast**
    halves (about 1 pound)
1   **can (10¾ ounces) condensed cream of**
    chicken soup
1   **soup can (1⅓ cups) water *or* milk**
2   **cups MINUTE White Rice, uncooked**

Heat oil in large nonstick skillet on medium-high heat. Add chicken; cover. Cook 4 minutes on each side or until cooked through. Remove chicken from skillet.

Add soup and water to skillet. Bring to boil.

Stir in rice. Top with chicken; cover. Cook on low heat 5 minutes. Garnish with fresh oregano.

***Note:** Increase oil to 2 tablespoons if using regular skillet.

Marinating Hints

To easily marinate chicken and steaks, freeze the poultry or meat right in a marinade. First, wash the pieces and pat dry. Then, place them in a large resealable plastic freezer bag with enough SEVEN SEAS VIVA Italian Dressing to coat, and place the bags in the freezer. To serve, thaw the pieces overnight in the refrigerator before cooking. The poultry or meat marinates as it thaws.

Oven *BBQ* Chicken

Prep time: 5 minutes   Baking time: 1 hour

Makes 4 servings

1   **broiler-fryer chicken, cut up (3 to 3½ pounds)**
1   **bottle (18 ounces) KRAFT Original Barbecue Sauce**

Place chicken in 13×9-inch baking dish.

Pour barbecue sauce over chicken.

Bake at 350°F, uncovered, for 1 hour or until cooked through.

Helpful Hint: For a quicker variation, substitute 6 boneless skinless chicken breast halves for broiler-fryer. Reduce barbecue sauce to 1 cup. Bake at 375°F, uncovered, for 25 minutes or until cooked through. Makes 6 servings.

Chicken Fanfare

Prep time: 15 minutes   Baking time: 40 minutes

Makes 6 servings

1	**package (6 ounces) STOVE TOP Stuffing Mix for Chicken**
1½	**cups water**
¼	**cup (½ stick) butter *or* margarine, melted**
1	**cup raisins**
6	**boneless skinless chicken breast halves (about 2 pounds)**
18	**slices OSCAR MAYER Center Cut Bacon**
½	**cup finely chopped pecans**

Mix Stuffing Crumbs, contents of Vegetable/Seasoning Packet, water, butter and raisins in 13×9-inch baking dish.

Wrap each chicken breast with 3 bacon slices. Place chicken over stuffing mixture. Sprinkle chicken with pecans.

Bake in upper third of oven at 375°F for 40 minutes or until chicken is cooked through.

Turkey and Green Bean Casserole

Prep time: 10 minutes   Baking time: 30 minutes

Makes 6 servings

1   **package (6 ounces) STOVE TOP Stuffing Mix for Chicken *or* Turkey**
1½   **cups hot water**
¼   **cup (½ stick) butter *or* margarine, cut into pieces**
3   **cups cubed cooked turkey *or* chicken**
1   **package (10 ounces) frozen French cut green beans, thawed**
1   **can (11 ounces) condensed cheddar cheese soup**
¾   **cup milk**

Mix contents of Vegetable/Seasoning Packet, hot water and butter in large bowl until butter is melted. Stir in Stuffing Crumbs just to moisten. Let stand 5 minutes.

Mix turkey and green beans in 2-quart casserole or 12×8-inch baking dish. Mix soup and milk in medium bowl until smooth; pour over turkey mixture. Spoon stuffing evenly over top.

Bake at 350°F for 30 minutes or until thoroughly heated.

STOVE TOP® One-Dish *Chicken Bake*

Prep time: 10 minutes   Baking time: 35 minutes

Makes 4 servings

1   package (6 ounces) STOVE TOP Stuffing
    Mix for Chicken
¼   cup (½ stick) butter *or* margarine, cut
    up
4   boneless skinless chicken breast halves
    (about 1¼ pounds)
1   can (10¾ ounces) condensed cream of
    mushroom soup
⅓   cup BREAKSTONE'S *or* KNUDSEN Sour
    Cream *or* milk

Mix contents of Vegetable/Seasoning Packet, Stuffing Crumbs, butter and 1½ cups hot water; set aside.

Place chicken in 13×9-inch baking dish or 2-quart casserole. Mix soup and sour cream; pour over chicken. Top with stuffing.

Bake at 375°F for 35 minutes or until chicken is cooked through.

Keep Chicken on Hand

Boneless, skinless chicken breasts are the base for so many dishes these days, it's smart to stock them in the freezer. Buy chicken breasts in a large, economical package. Clean and freeze them in packages of four or in amounts for your favorite recipe. Set the frozen chicken in the refrigerator first thing in the morning. It'll be thawed by the time you need to cook dinner.

TACO BELL® HOME ORIGINALS®
2-Step Tacos
Makes 6 servings

You only need:
- 1 **pound ground beef**
- 1 **package (1.25 ounces) TACO BELL HOME ORIGINALS Taco Seasoning Mix**
- 1 **package (4.5 ounces) TACO BELL HOME ORIGINALS Taco Shells**
  KRAFT Shredded Cheese
  TACO BELL HOME ORIGINALS Thick 'N Chunky Salsa
  Packaged cut-up lettuce

1. Prep it quick! Cook meat; drain. Add seasoning mix; prepare as directed on package.

2. Pile on the fun!™ Place bowls of cooked meat and remaining ingredients on your table. Pass the heated taco shells and let everyone build their own!

Note: You can substitute 1 package (10.75 ounces) TACO BELL HOME ORIGINALS Taco Dinner Kit for the seasoning mix, taco shells and salsa. It's all in the kit!

TACO BELL and HOME ORIGINALS are registered trademarks owned and licensed by Taco Bell Corp.

Taco Serve-Alongs

Here's a neat way to serve taco toppings: Place the cheese, salsa and lettuce in the separate cups of a muffin tin. This way there's only one item to pass around the table. A muffin tin also works great for holding condiments for hamburgers and hot dogs.

Cheesy Chicken Fajitas

Prep time: 15 minutes   Cooking time: 10 minutes

Makes 6 servings

½   **pound boneless skinless chicken breasts, cut into thin strips**
1   **clove garlic, minced**
1   **medium green *and/or* red pepper, cut into strips**
½   **cup sliced onion**
1½   **cups KRAFT Four Cheese Mexican Style Shredded Cheese**
6   **flour tortillas (6-inch), warmed**
    TACO BELL HOME ORIGINALS Thick 'N Chunky Salsa

Spray skillet with no stick cooking spray. Add chicken and garlic; cook on medium-high heat 5 minutes.

Add green pepper and onion; cook 4 to 5 minutes or until tender-crisp.

Place ¼ cup chicken mixture and ¼ cup cheese on center of each tortilla; fold. Serve with salsa and lime wedges.

TACO BELL and HOME ORIGINALS are registered trademarks owned and licensed by Taco Bell Corp.

Chicken Sour Cream *Enchiladas*

Prep time: 20 minutes   Baking time: 35 minutes

Makes 5 servings

1   container (16 ounces) BREAKSTONE'S *or* KNUDSEN Sour Cream, divided
2   cups chopped cooked chicken
1   package (8 ounces) KRAFT Natural *or* ⅓ Less Fat Shredded Reduced Fat Colby and Monterey Jack Cheese, divided
1   cup TACO BELL HOME ORIGINALS Thick 'N Chunky Salsa, divided
2   tablespoons chopped cilantro
1   teaspoon ground cumin
10 flour tortillas (6-inch)
1   cup shredded lettuce
½   cup chopped tomato

Mix 1 cup of the sour cream, chicken, 1 cup of the cheese, ¼ cup of the salsa, cilantro and cumin.

Spoon about ¼ cup of the chicken mixture down center of each tortilla; roll up. Place in 13×9-inch baking dish. Top with remaining ¾ cup salsa; cover.

Bake at 350°F for 30 minutes. Sprinkle with remaining 1 cup cheese. Bake an additional 5 minutes or until cheese is melted. Top with lettuce and tomato. Serve with remaining 1 cup sour cream.

TACO BELL and HOME ORIGINALS are registered trademarks owned and licensed by Taco Bell Corp.

Quick Taco Quesadillas

Prep time: 10 minutes   Baking time: 10 minutes

Makes 5 main-dish servings or cut each tortilla into thirds for 30 appetizer servings

1 **pound ground beef**
1 **package (16.33 ounces) TACO BELL HOME ORIGINALS Soft Taco Dinner Kit**
2 **avocados, peeled, sliced (optional)**
1 **package (8 ounces) KRAFT Finely Shredded Cheddar Cheese**

Brown meat; drain. Add Seasoning Mix; prepare as directed on package.

Soften Tortillas as directed on package. Spoon meat mixture over bottom halves of tortillas. Top with avocados and cheese. Drizzle with Taco Sauce. Fold tortillas in half; place on cookie sheet sprayed with no stick cooking spray.

Bake at 425°F for 8 to 10 minutes. Serve warm with hot sauce, if desired.

Make-ahead tip: Prepare as directed except do not bake; cover. Refrigerate up to 6 hours. When ready to serve, bake, uncovered, at 425°F for 15 to 20 minutes or until thoroughly heated.

TACO BELL and HOME ORIGINALS are registered trademarks owned and licensed by Taco Bell Corp.

Cheeseburger Rice

Prep time: 10 minutes   Cooking time: 15 minutes

Makes 4 servings

1	**pound lean ground beef**
1¾	**cups water**
⅔	**cup catsup**
1	**tablespoon prepared mustard**
2	**cups MINUTE White Rice, uncooked**
1	**cup KRAFT Shredded Cheddar Cheese**

Brown meat in large skillet on medium-high heat; drain.

Add water, catsup and mustard. Bring to boil.

Stir in rice. Sprinkle with cheese; cover. Cook on low heat 5 minutes.

Cheesy Chili Fries

Prep time: 20 minutes   Microwave time: 2 minutes

Makes 6 to 8 servings

1 **package (32 ounces) frozen French fried potatoes**

1 **can (15 ounces) chili, heated as directed on label**

1 **jar (16 ounces) CHEEZ WHIZ Pasteurized Process Cheese Sauce**

Prepare potatoes as directed on package.

Arrange potatoes on large serving platter. Pour hot chili over potatoes.

Microwave process cheese sauce as directed on label. Pour process cheese sauce over chili.

Easy Pleasing *Meatloaf*

Prep time: 10 minutes   Baking time: 1 hour

Makes 6 to 8 servings

2 **pounds lean ground beef *or* turkey**
1 **cup water**
1 **package (6¼ ounces) STOVE TOP Stuffing Mix for Beef**
2 **eggs, beaten**
½ **cup KRAFT Original Barbecue Sauce, divided**

Mix all ingredients except ¼ cup of the barbecue sauce.

Shape meat mixture into oval loaf in 13×9-inch baking dish; top with remaining ¼ cup barbecue sauce.

Bake at 375°F for 1 hour or until center is no longer pink. Garnish with chopped fresh thyme.

Italian *Pork Chops* Mozzarella

Prep time: 10 minutes   Baking time: 25 minutes

Makes 8 servings

8   **boneless pork chops (½ inch thick)**
1   **packet SHAKE 'N BAKE Seasoned Coating
     Mix Original Pork**
1½ **cups spaghetti sauce**
1   **cup KRAFT Shredded Low-Moisture
     Part-Skim Mozzarella Cheese**

Moisten chops with water. Shake off excess.

Shake or coat 1 or 2 chops at a time with coating mix. Discard any remaining mix. Place in 15×10×1-inch baking pan.

Bake at 425°F for 15 minutes or until cooked through. Top chops with spaghetti sauce and cheese. Bake an additional 10 minutes or until sauce is warm and cheese is melted.

Home-Style *Tuna* Casserole

Prep time: 15 minutes   Baking time: 35 minutes

Makes 4 servings

1   package (14 ounces) KRAFT Deluxe
    Macaroni & Cheese Dinner *or* KRAFT
    Light Deluxe Macaroni & Cheese
    Dinner
1   can (10¾ ounces) condensed cream of
    celery soup
1   can (6 ounces) tuna, drained, flaked
1   cup frozen peas
½   cup milk
2   tablespoons finely chopped onion
2   cups fresh bread crumbs
¼   cup (½ stick) butter *or* margarine,
    melted

Prepare Dinner as directed on package.
Add soup, tuna, peas, milk and onion;
mix lightly.

Spoon into 2-quart casserole. Toss crumbs
and butter; sprinkle over casserole.

Bake at 350°F for 30 to 35 minutes or
until thoroughly heated.

SEVEN SEAS® *Simply Marinade*

Prep time: 5 minutes plus marinating   Grilling time: 18 minutes

Makes 4 to 6 servings

**1   cup SEVEN SEAS VIVA Italian Dressing,
      divided**

1½   pounds fish and vegetables

Pour ¾ cup of the dressing over fish and vegetables; cover.

Refrigerate 30 minutes to 1 hour to marinate. Drain; discard dressing.

Place fish and vegetables on greased grill over medium coals or on rack of broiler pan 4 to 6 inches from heat. Grill or broil to desired doneness, turning and brushing with remaining ¼ cup dressing. Garnish with fresh tarragon and dill flower.

Zuppa di Pesce

Prep time: 15 minutes   Cooking time: 25 minutes

Makes 4 to 6 servings

¼ cup olive oil
1 medium onion, chopped
2 cloves garlic, minced
1 can (28 ounces) Italian-style plum
   tomatoes, undrained
½ cup dry white wine
2 tablespoons julienne-cut fresh basil
   leaves
2 pounds soft-flesh fish fillets (such as
   cod, red snapper, orange roughy *or* a
   mixture), cut into chunks
   DI GIORNO Shredded Parmesan Cheese

Heat oil in large saucepan. Add onion and garlic; cook and stir 4 to 5 minutes or until tender.

Stir in tomatoes, wine and basil, breaking up tomatoes with back of spoon. Bring to a boil. Reduce heat to medium-low; cook, uncovered, 10 minutes.

Add fish. Simmer 10 minutes or until fish flakes easily with fork. Ladle into serving bowls. Sprinkle with cheese. Garnish with additional julienne-cut fresh basil leaves.

Mincing Garlic

There are several ways to mince garlic quickly and easily. You can use a garlic press to crush the clove, smash it by placing a flat side of a chef's knife over the clove and hitting it with the side of your fist, or cut a peeled clove into tiny pieces with a sharp knife. For real convenience, look for bottled minced garlic in your supermarket produce section.

Double Cheese Chili
(recipe opposite page)

Easy Wrap Sandwiches
(recipe, page 177)

Double Cheese *Chili*

Prep time: 10 minutes   Cooking time: 30 minutes

Makes 6 servings

1   pound LOUIS RICH Ground Turkey, thawed, *or ground beef*
½   cup *each* chopped onion and chopped green pepper
1   can (15 ounces) kidney beans, drained
1   can (14½ ounces) whole tomatoes, undrained
1   can (8 ounces) tomato sauce
1   tablespoon chili powder
    KRAFT Finely Shredded Mild Cheddar Cheese

Brown turkey in large skillet on medium heat until no longer pink; drain. Add onion and green pepper; cook until tender.

Stir in beans, tomatoes, tomato sauce and chili powder; cover. Simmer on low heat 30 minutes, stirring occasionally.

Sprinkle cheese in bottom of serving bowls. Spoon chili over cheese; sprinkle with additional cheese. Top with BREAKSTONE'S or KNUDSEN Sour Cream, if desired. Garnish with chopped fresh parsley or cilantro.

Bread with Zing

For a flavorful and crispy bread fix-up to accompany soups and a variety of other main dishes, prepare your favorite GOOD SEASONS Salad Dressing Mix and brush some dressing on French bread slices. Then, toast the slices as you would garlic bread.

Chunky Chicken Vegetable Soup

Prep time: 10 minutes   Cooking time: 20 minutes plus standing

Makes about 5 cups

½   **pound boneless skinless chicken breasts, cubed**
1   **can (13¾ ounces) chicken broth**
1½   **cups water**
2   **cups assorted cut-up fresh vegetables, such as sliced carrots, broccoli flowerets and chopped red pepper, *or* 1 package (10 ounces) frozen mixed vegetables, thawed**
1   **envelope GOOD SEASONS Italian Salad Dressing Mix**
½   **cup MINUTE White Rice, uncooked**

Cook and stir chicken in large saucepan sprayed with no stick cooking spray until cooked through, about 8 minutes.

Stir in broth, water, vegetables and salad dressing mix. Bring to boil. Reduce heat to low; cover. Simmer 7 to 9 minutes or until vegetables are tender. (If using frozen vegetables, simmer 5 minutes.)

Stir in rice; cover. Remove from heat. Let stand 5 minutes.

Chicken 'n Peppers Pasta Skillet

Prep time: 10 minutes   Cooking time: 10 minutes plus standing

Makes 6 servings

1   **pound boneless skinless chicken breasts, chopped**
1   **green pepper, cut into thin strips**
1   **jar (14 ounces) spaghetti sauce (about 1½ cups)**
2   **cups (4 ounces) rotini pasta, cooked, drained**
2   **cups KRAFT Classic Garlic Italian Style Shredded Cheese, divided**

Spray large skillet with no stick cooking spray. Add chicken; cook and stir 5 minutes. Add green pepper; cook and stir until chicken is cooked through and green pepper is tender.

Stir in sauce, rotini and 1 cup of the cheese. Sprinkle with remaining 1 cup cheese; cover. Let stand 1 to 2 minutes or until cheese is melted.

Shells with *Tomato & Basil*

Prep time: 5 minutes   Cooking time: 15 minutes

Makes 6 to 8 servings

1   **package (12 ounces) VELVEETA Shells & Cheese Dinner**

1   **tomato, chopped**

2   **tablespoons julienne-cut fresh basil leaves *or* ½ teaspoon dried basil**

½   **teaspoon garlic powder**

Prepare VELVEETA Shells & Cheese Dinner as directed on package.

Stir in remaining ingredients; cook until thoroughly heated.

Cheesy *Primavera* Mac Skillet

Prep time: 15 minutes   Cooking time: 15 minutes

Makes 5 servings

2⅓   **cups water**
1   **package (14 ounces) KRAFT Deluxe Macaroni & Cheese Dinner *or* KRAFT Light Deluxe Macaroni & Cheese Dinner**
½   **teaspoon dried basil leaves, crushed**
½   **teaspoon garlic powder**
3   **cups frozen vegetable medley (broccoli, cauliflower and carrots)**

Bring water to boil in large skillet. Stir in Macaroni and seasonings; return to boil.

Stir in vegetables. Reduce heat to medium-low; cover. Simmer 10 minutes or until Macaroni is tender.

Stir in Cheese Sauce. Cook and stir 2 minutes on medium-high heat until thickened and creamy. Season to taste with salt and pepper, if desired. Garnish with green onion curls and tomato wedge.

VELVEETA® *Cheeseburger Mac*

Prep time: 10 minutes   Cooking time: 15 minutes

Makes 4 to 6 servings

1	**pound ground beef**
2¾	**cups water**
⅓	**cup catsup**
1	**to 2 teaspoons onion powder**
2	**cups elbow macaroni, uncooked**
¾	**pound (12 ounces) VELVEETA Pasteurized Process Cheese Spread, cut up**

Brown meat in large skillet; drain.

Stir in water, catsup and onion powder. Bring to boil. Stir in macaroni. Reduce heat to medium-low; cover. Simmer 8 to 10 minutes or until macaroni is tender.

Add process cheese spread; stir until melted.

Saucepan *Turkey* Tetrazzini

Prep time: 10 minutes   Cooking time: 15 minutes

Makes 6 servings

1   **package (14 ounces) KRAFT Deluxe Macaroni & Cheese Dinner**
1   **cup sliced onion**
2   **cups chopped cooked turkey**
1   **can (4 ounces) sliced mushrooms, drained**
⅓   **cup milk**
½   **teaspoon poultry seasoning**
1   **tablespoon chopped fresh parsley (optional)**

Prepare Macaroni & Cheese Dinner as directed on package, adding onion during last 5 minutes of pasta cooking time.

Stir in remaining ingredients. Heat thoroughly. Garnish with red pepper strips and fresh basil.

Cheesy Chicken & Broccoli Macaroni

Prep time: 10 minutes   Cooking time: 15 minutes

Makes 6 servings

4   boneless skinless chicken breast halves
    (about 1¼ pounds), cut into chunks
1   can (13¾ ounces) chicken broth
1   package (7 ounces) elbow macaroni,
    uncooked
¾   pound (12 ounces) VELVEETA Pasteurized
    Process Cheese Spread, cut up
1   package (10 ounces) frozen chopped
    broccoli, thawed

Spray large skillet with no stick cooking spray. Add chicken; cook and stir 2 minutes or until chicken is no longer pink.

Stir in broth. Bring to boil. Stir in macaroni. Reduce heat to medium-low; cover. Simmer 8 to 10 minutes or until macaroni is tender.

Add process cheese spread and broccoli; stir until process cheese spread is melted.

Easy Skillet *Frittata*

Prep time: 15 minutes   Cooking time: 16 minutes

Makes 6 servings

3 tablespoons oil
2 cups frozen shredded hash brown
   potatoes
½ green pepper, chopped
6 eggs, beaten
2 tablespoons milk *or* water
10 slices OSCAR MAYER Center Cut Bacon,
   cut into 1-inch pieces, cooked, drained
½ cup KRAFT Shredded Sharp Cheddar
   Cheese

Heat oil in large nonstick skillet. Add potatoes and pepper; cook 5 minutes or until potatoes are browned, stirring often.

Mix eggs and milk. Pour mixture evenly over potatoes and green pepper; sprinkle with bacon. Cover. Reduce heat to low. Cook 8 to 11 minutes or until eggs are set.

Sprinkle with cheese. Cover. Heat until cheese melts. Cut into wedges.

Applesauce Muffins

Prep time: 20 minutes   Baking time: 20 minutes

Makes 12

1 cup flour
⅓ cup firmly packed brown sugar
2 teaspoons CALUMET Baking Powder
¼ teaspoon ground cinnamon
¼ teaspoon salt
2 cups POST GREAT GRAINS Cereal, any
   variety
1 cup skim milk
1 egg
1 cup chunky applesauce
2 tablespoons oil

Mix flour, sugar, baking powder, cinnamon and salt in large bowl. Mix cereal and milk in another bowl. Let stand 3 minutes. Stir in egg, applesauce and oil. Add to flour mixture; stir just until moistened. (Batter will be lumpy.)

Spoon batter into muffin pan sprayed with no stick cooking spray, filling each cup ⅔ full.

Bake at 400°F for 20 minutes or until golden brown. Serve warm.

Blueberry Pancakes

Prep time: 10 minutes plus standing   Cooking time: 10 minutes

Makes 8 pancakes or 4 servings

1   **egg**
¾   **cup milk**
2   **teaspoons oil**
1   **cup pancake and waffle mix**
1   **cup POST GREAT GRAINS Whole Grain Cereal**

Beat egg in large bowl; stir in milk and oil. Add pancake mix; stir just until moistened. Stir in cereal. Let stand 5 minutes.

Pour ¼ cup batter onto hot griddle for each pancake; cook until bubbles form on top. Turn to brown other side. Garnish with fresh blueberries and raspberries and sprinkle with powdered sugar.

GOOD TO THE LAST DROP® Coffee

Brewing that perfect cup of coffee is easy when you remember five basic rules:
1. Always start with cold water.
2. Be precise with measuring. Use one rounded tablespoon for each six fluid ounces.
3. Serve it freshly brewed.
4. Store ground coffee in a tightly sealed container in your refrigerator or freezer.
5. Clean your coffeemaker regularly.

Greek Pita Sandwiches
(recipe, page 78)

SPEEDY SANDWICHES & MAIN-DISH SALADS

For satisfying meals that are ready in minutes, it's hard to beat these two-fisted sandwiches and enticing main-dish salads. Delights, such as Country Ham Sandwiches, Grilled Turkey Club, Ranch Taco Chicken Salad and Summertime Tuna Pasta Salad, make for sensational, carefree dining no matter how hectic your schedule.

Greek *Pita* Sandwiches

(Photo on pages 76–77.)

Prep time: 10 minutes

Makes 6 servings

1 **pound chopped cooked chicken**
½ **cup olive oil**
½ **cup chopped tomato**
1 **package (4 ounces) ATHENOS Crumbled Feta Cheese**
1 **can (2¼ ounces) sliced pitted ripe olives, drained**
1 **envelope GOOD SEASONS Italian *or* Zesty Italian Salad Dressing Mix**
6 **pita breads**

Mix all ingredients except pita breads in medium bowl.

Top half of each pita bread with ½ cup chicken mixture.

Fold pita breads. Secure with wooden toothpicks.

Cooked Chicken Choices

Don't have leftover cooked chicken to make Greek Pita Sandwiches? Just look in the freezer section of your supermarket for frozen cooked chicken. Or, stop by the deli counter and purchase a whole roasted bird. Remove the meat from the bones and dice it. Use 1 pound for the sandwiches and freeze the rest for next time.

Mediterranean *Wrap* Sandwiches

Prep time: 10 minutes plus refrigerating

Makes 8 sandwiches

½ **cup MIRACLE WHIP *or* MIRACLE WHIP LIGHT Dressing**
½ **teaspoon *each* dried oregano leaves and garlic powder**
8 **flour tortillas (8-inch)**
2 **packages (5.5 ounces *each*) LOUIS RICH CARVING BOARD Oven Roasted Turkey Breast**
1 **cup cucumber strips**
1 **red pepper, cut into strips (optional)**

Mix dressing and seasonings. Spread on tortillas.

Top with turkey, cucumber and red pepper; roll up.

Wrap in plastic wrap. Refrigerate until ready to serve.

Helpful Hint: For bite-size snacks or appetizers, cut rolls into 1-inch pieces.

BBQ *Chicken Wrap* Sandwiches

Prep time: 15 minutes   Grilling time: 12 minutes

Makes 4 servings

1   **pound boneless skinless chicken breasts**
2   **medium green peppers, quartered**
1   **medium onion, sliced**
1   **cup KRAFT Original Barbecue Sauce**
8   **flour tortillas (6-inch) *or* 4 flour tortillas (10-inch), warmed**

Place chicken and vegetables on greased grill over medium-hot coals.

Grill chicken 10 to 12 minutes or until cooked through and vegetables 8 to 10 minutes, brushing each frequently with sauce and turning occasionally.

Slice chicken and vegetables into thin strips. Divide filling among tortillas. Fold up sides of tortilla to center, slightly overlapping. Secure with toothpick, if desired. Serve with additional sauce, if desired.

BBQ Pork Wrap Sandwiches: Prepare sandwiches as directed, substituting boneless pork chops for chicken. Grill 16 minutes or until cooked through, turning occasionally.

Western *Bologna* Sub

Prep time: 10 minutes

Makes 4 servings

1   **small loaf (8 ounces) French *or*
    sourdough bread, cut in half
    lengthwise**
2   **tablespoons KRAFT Mayo Real
    Mayonnaise**
2   **tablespoons KRAFT Original Barbecue
    Sauce
    Leaf lettuce**
1   **package (8 ounces) OSCAR MAYER
    Bologna
    Thinly sliced onion**
4   **slices OSCAR MAYER Bacon, crisply
    cooked**

Spread bottom half of bread loaf with
mayo. Spread top half of bread loaf with
barbecue sauce.

Layer bottom with lettuce, bologna, onion,
bacon and additional lettuce. Cover with
top half of bread. Cut into 4 pieces. Secure
with garnished toothpick, if desired.

Decorative Picks

Instead of purchasing decorative picks, make your own to add a special touch to
sandwiches and appetizers. To make them, use small cookie cutters or, for simple
shapes, a paring knife to cut shapes from strips of red, orange, yellow or green
pepper or citrus peel. Then, just slide the shapes onto wooden or plastic picks.

STOVE TOP® and *Roasted Turkey* Sandwich

Prep time: 20 minutes

Makes 4 open-face sandwiches

1 **package (6 ounces) STOVE TOP
   Cranberry Stuffing Mix**
4 **slices bread**
1 **pound LOUIS RICH Breast of Turkey, cut
   into 12 slices**
1 **cup hot gravy**

Prepare stuffing mix as directed on package; set aside.

Arrange 1 bread slice on each of 4 individual plates. Top each with 3 turkey slices, ¾ cup hot stuffing and ¼ cup gravy. Microwave each sandwich on HIGH 30 seconds, if necessary.

Serve with cranberry sauce and steamed whole green beans, if desired.

All American Deluxe Cheeseburgers

Prep time: 10 minutes   Grilling time: 12 minutes

Makes 4 sandwiches

1   **pound ground beef**
8   **KRAFT Deluxe Process American Cheese Slices**
2   **tablespoons KRAFT Thousand Island Dressing**
2   **tablespoons KRAFT Mayo Real Mayonnaise**
4   **Kaiser *or* hamburger rolls, split, toasted**
    Lettuce
    Tomato and red onion slices
    CLAUSSEN Classic Dill Super Slices for Burgers

Shape meat into 4 patties. Place patties on grill over hot coals. Grill 8 to 12 minutes or to desired doneness, turning occasionally.

Top each patty with 2 process cheese slices; cover. Continue grilling until process cheese is melted.

Mix dressing and mayo in small bowl. Spread 1 tablespoon dressing mixture on each roll. Fill rolls with cheeseburgers, lettuce, tomato, onion and pickles.

Grilled *Turkey* Club

Prep time: 5 minutes   Cooking time: 10 minutes

Makes 1 sandwich

2   **slices bread**
2   **KRAFT Singles Process Cheese Food**
       Tomato slices
4   **slices LOUIS RICH CARVING BOARD Thin**
       Carved Oven Roasted Turkey Breast
2   **slices OSCAR MAYER Bacon, crisply**
       cooked
       Butter *or* margarine, softened

Top 1 bread slice with 1 process cheese food slice, tomato, turkey, bacon, second process cheese food slice and second bread slice.

Spread outside of sandwich with butter.

Cook in skillet on medium heat until lightly browned on both sides. Cut into triangles. Secure with toothpicks, if desired.

Double-Duty Bacon

When you're cooking OSCAR MAYER Bacon, sizzle some extra slices. Drain on paper towels. Crumble and refrigerate or freeze in a tightly sealed storage bag. Next time you're in a hurry, stir the cooked bacon pieces into grits, pancakes or scrambled eggs.

Garden Tuna Melts

Prep time: 10 minutes   Cooking time: 10 minutes

Makes 4 sandwiches

1   **can (6 ounces) white tuna in water, drained, flaked**
⅓   **cup KRAFT Mayo Real Mayonnaise *or* MIRACLE WHIP Salad Dressing**
¼   **cup *each* chopped onion and green pepper**
½   **teaspoon *each* dried basil leaves and dried oregano leaves**
8   **slices bread**
4   **KRAFT Singles Process Cheese Food**

Mix tuna, mayo, onion, green pepper and seasonings.

Top 4 bread slices each with 1 process cheese food slice, tuna mixture and second bread slice. Spread outsides of sandwiches with additional mayo or softened butter.

Cook in skillet on medium heat until lightly browned on both sides.

Round Out the Meal

Here are some handy ways, using KRAFT products, to turn a simple sandwich into a complete meal:

• Serve your favorite KRAFT dressing with 1 package (10 ounces) mixed salad greens or pre-cut carrots and celery sticks.
• Pour heated CHEEZ WHIZ Pasteurized Process Cheese Sauce over steamed cut-up broccoli.
• For an easy ready-to-eat dessert, try JELL-O Gelatin Snacks or JELL-O Pudding Snacks. For an added treat, stir chopped nuts, granola, chopped candy bars or fruit into the pudding snacks.

Creamy Tuna *Caesar* Sub

Prep time: 20 minutes

Makes 4 servings

½ cup KRAFT Mayo: Real *or* Light Mayonnaise

½ cup KRAFT Caesar Italian Dressing *or* KRAFT Ranch Dressing

½ cup (2 ounces) KRAFT 100% Grated Parmesan Cheese

2 cans (6 ounces *each*) tuna, drained, flaked

1 loaf French bread, cut in half lengthwise

2 cups torn romaine lettuce

1 large tomato, thinly sliced

1 small red onion, thinly sliced (optional)

Mix mayo, dressing and cheese. Add tuna; mix lightly.

Top bottom of bread loaf with lettuce, tomato, onion, tuna mixture and top half of bread loaf. Cut into 4 pieces.

Variation: Substitute 4 Italian bread rolls (6-inch), split, for French bread loaf.

Country Ham Sandwiches

Prep time: 10 minutes

Makes 4 sandwiches

½   **cup MIRACLE WHIP Salad Dressing *or* KRAFT Mayo Real Mayonnaise**

½   **teaspoon garlic powder**

½   **teaspoon pepper**

8   **slices whole wheat bread
Lettuce and tomato slices (optional)**

1   **package (6 ounces) OSCAR MAYER Smoked Cooked Ham**

8   **KRAFT Singles Process Cheese Food**

Mix salad dressing and seasonings in small bowl.

Spread on bread slices.

Layer 4 of the bread slices each with lettuce, tomato, ham and 2 process cheese food slices. Top with second bread slices.

Super *Roast Beef* Sandwiches

Prep time: 10 minutes

Makes 4 sandwiches

1	cup MIRACLE WHIP *or* MIRACLE WHIP LIGHT Dressing
1	cup BREAKSTONE'S *or* KNUDSEN Sour Cream
2	teaspoons dill weed
1	teaspoon onion powder
1	round focaccia bread (8-inch)
	Lettuce leaves
	Tomato slices
¾	pound deli sliced roast beef

Mix dressing, sour cream and seasonings.

Cut focaccia bread into 4 pieces; split. Spread cut surfaces of bread with dressing mixture.

Fill with lettuce, tomato and meat.

Helpful Hint: Refrigerate remaining dressing mixture. Serve with assorted cut-up vegetables or spread on turkey sandwiches.

Cheezy Dogs

Prep time: 5 minutes   Grilling time: 6 minutes

Makes 8 sandwiches

1   **package (16 ounces) OSCAR MAYER
    Bun-Length Beef Franks *or* Wieners**
8   **hot dog buns**
1   **cup CHEEZ WHIZ Pasteurized Process
    Cheese Sauce, microwaved as
    directed on label**

Grill franks 6 minutes or until
heated through.

Place franks in buns. Drizzle about
2 tablespoons process cheese sauce over
each frank.

Ranch Taco Chicken Salad

Prep time: 15 minutes   Cooking time: 8 minutes

Makes 6 servings

1   **pound boneless skinless chicken breasts, cut into strips**
1   **cup TACO BELL HOME ORIGINALS Thick 'N Chunky Salsa, divided**
1   **package (16 ounces) salad greens**
1   **cup KRAFT Shredded Cheddar Cheese**
1   **cup KRAFT FREE Ranch Fat Free Dressing *or* KRAFT Ranch Dressing**

Cook and stir chicken in ¼ cup of the salsa in large nonstick skillet on medium-high heat 8 minutes or until chicken is cooked through.

Toss chicken, greens and cheese on serving platter or in large bowl.

Top with remaining ¾ cup salsa and dressing before serving. Garnish with tortilla chips.

Spicy Ranch Taco Chicken Salad:
Prepare salad as directed, adding 1 tablespoon chili powder to salsa while cooking chicken.

TACO BELL and HOME ORIGINALS are registered trademarks owned and licensed by Taco Bell Corp.

Make a Sandwich

Turning Ranch Taco Chicken Salad into wrap sandwiches is simple. Just fill burrito wraps with the tossed ingredients and roll up—it's so easy! For a change of pace, pair the salad mixture with flavored burrito wraps—like herb, tomato and spinach.

Raspberry Chicken Salad

Prep time: 10 minutes

Makes 6 servings

1 **package (16 ounces) mixed salad greens *or* spinach**
2 **cups sliced grilled *or* broiled chicken**
¾ **cup SEVEN SEAS FREE Raspberry Vinaigrette Fat Free Dressing**
½ **cup walnut pieces *or* chow mein noodles (optional)**

Place greens on large platter or in large bowl.

Top with remaining ingredients. Garnish with fresh raspberries.

Ranch *Chicken* Pasta Salad

Prep time: 25 minutes

Makes 4 (1 cup) servings

1   **package (10.4 ounces) KRAFT Classic
    Ranch with Bacon Pasta Salad**
1   **cup chopped cooked chicken *or* turkey**
1   **cup chopped tomatoes**
¼   **cup sliced green onions**

Prepare Pasta Salad as directed
on package.

Stir in remaining ingredients. Refrigerate
or serve immediately. Garnish with
fresh herbs.

Fruity Chicken Salad

Prep time: 10 minutes plus refrigerating

Makes 6 servings

1 **envelope GOOD SEASONS Honey, French** **or Italian Salad Dressing Mix**
¼ **cup red wine vinegar**
3 **cups cooked orzo pasta**
2 **cups chopped cooked chicken**
1 **cup red and green seedless grapes**
½ **cup thin carrot strips**
 Chopped fresh parsley

Prepare dressing in cruet or small bowl as directed on envelope using red wine vinegar for the vinegar.

Mix orzo, chicken, grapes and carrot in large bowl. Add ½ cup of the dressing; toss to mix well. Cover.

Refrigerate salad and remaining dressing at least 2 hours. Just before serving, mix in remaining dressing. Serve on lettuce-lined plate. Sprinkle with parsley.

Southwestern *Grilled Chicken* Salad

Prep time: 20 minutes

Makes 4 servings

8   cups shredded lettuce
1   pound boneless skinless chicken breast
     halves, grilled, sliced
1   cup KRAFT Four Cheese Mexican Style
     Shredded Cheese
1   large tomato, cut into wedges
½   cup canned black beans, drained,
     rinsed
¼   cup sliced green onions

Arrange all ingredients on large
serving platter.

Serve with KRAFT Ranch Dressing or salsa.

Chicken Salad

Prep time: 15 minutes plus refrigerating

Makes 4 servings

4   **boneless skinless chicken breast halves (about 1¼ pounds), cooked, cubed**
1   **cup red grapes**
¾   **cup MIRACLE WHIP *or* MIRACLE WHIP LIGHT Dressing**
1   **teaspoon dried tarragon leaves**

Mix all ingredients. Refrigerate several hours or overnight. Serve on lettuce leaves, if desired. Garnish with fresh tarragon.

CATALINA® *Berry* Chicken Salad

Prep time: 20 minutes   Cooking time: 8 minutes

Makes 4 servings

1   **pound boneless skinless chicken breasts, cut into strips**
1   **cup KRAFT FREE CATALINA Fat Free Dressing *or* KRAFT CATALINA Dressing, divided**
1   **package (10 ounces) salad greens *or* spinach**
1   **cup sliced strawberries**
¼   **cup sliced almonds**

Cook chicken in ¼ cup of the dressing in medium skillet on medium heat 8 minutes or until cooked through.

Toss greens, strawberries, almonds and chicken in large salad bowl. Drizzle with remaining ¾ cup dressing. Toss.

Grilled Chicken Caesar Salad

Prep time: 15 minutes

Makes 6 servings

8   **cups torn romaine lettuce *or* 1 package (10 ounces) mixed *or* romaine salad greens**
1   **pound boneless skinless chicken breasts, grilled, cut into strips**
1   **cup seasoned croutons**
½   **cup (2 ounces) KRAFT 100% Shredded *or* Grated Parmesan Cheese**
¾   **cup KRAFT Classic Caesar Dressing *or* KRAFT Caesar Italian Dressing***

Toss lettuce, chicken, croutons and cheese in large salad bowl with dressing.

Serve with fresh lemon wedges and fresh ground pepper, if desired. Garnish with curled lemon peel and tomato wedges.

***Note:** KRAFT FREE Classic Caesar Fat Free Dressing or KRAFT FREE Caesar Italian Fat Free Dressing can be substituted for regular dressing.

Grilled Chicken Caesar Salad with Garlic: Prepare salad as directed, except cut garlic clove in half; rub cut edges on inside of serving bowl before adding greens.

Grilled Chicken Mediterranean-Style Salad: Prepare salad as directed. Toss salad with pitted ripe olives or plum tomato wedges.

Grilled Chicken
Caesar Salad
(recipe opposite page)

Grilled Bread
(recipe, page 141)

Bacon *Spinach* Salad

Prep time: 15 minutes

Makes 6 servings

5   cups torn spinach
1   cup sliced mushrooms
½   cup thinly sliced red onion wedges
4   slices OSCAR MAYER Bacon, crisply
      cooked, crumbled
2   hard-cooked eggs, chopped
1   cup KRAFT CATALINA Dressing

Toss all ingredients except dressing in large bowl. Serve with dressing.

Chicken and Bacon Spinach Salad:
Prepare salad as directed, adding
2 boneless skinless chicken breasts, grilled,
cut into strips.

Summertime Tuna Pasta Salad

Prep time: 25 minutes plus refrigerating

Makes 6 servings

2 cups pasta (such as bow ties, mafalda *or* macaroni), cooked, drained

1 can (6 ounces) white tuna in water, drained, flaked

1 cup MIRACLE WHIP *or* MIRACLE WHIP LIGHT Dressing

1 cup *each* broccoli flowerets, chopped carrots and sliced celery *or* chopped seeded cucumber

1 teaspoon dill weed

½ teaspoon pepper

Mix all ingredients. Refrigerate several hours or overnight. Serve on lettuce-lined platter. Garnish with halved lemon slices.

Meat and *Potatoes* Salad

Prep time: 10 minutes plus marinating   Grilling time: 15 minutes

Makes 4 servings

1½ cups SEVEN SEAS VIVA Italian Dressing, divided
1 pound beef sirloin steak
½ pound new potatoes, cut into quarters
1 package (10 ounces) mixed salad greens
1 cup tomato wedges
½ cup thinly sliced red onion

Pour 1 cup of the dressing over steak; cover. Refrigerate 4 hours or overnight to marinate. Drain; discard dressing.

Place potatoes in double layer of heavy-duty aluminum foil to form pouch; top with remaining ½ cup dressing.

Grill steak and potato pouch over medium coals 15 minutes or to desired doneness. Cut steak across grain into thin strips. Toss greens, tomato, onion, steak strips and potatoes. Toss with additional dressing, if desired.

Grilling Tips

Grilling is one of the easiest and most pleasant ways to cook. To ensure great results, follow these hints:
• Always make sure the grill rack is clean before grilling.
• To prevent foods from sticking to the grill rack during cooking, spray the unheated rack away from the fire with no stick cooking spray or brush with oil.
• Use tongs or a metal spatula to move and turn meat on the grill rather than using a fork. Piercing the meat with a fork causes the juices to escape, which makes the meat less flavorful and less moist.

Easy *Ham* Layered Salad

Prep time: 15 minutes plus refrigerating

Makes 8 servings

1   **package (10 ounces) mixed salad greens**
6   **plum tomatoes, chopped**
8   **CLAUSSEN Mini Kosher Dill Pickles, chopped**
4   **hard-cooked eggs, chopped**
2   **cups cubed ham**
1   **small red onion, chopped**
1   **bottle (8 ounces) KRAFT Peppercorn Ranch Dressing**

Place greens in bottom of large salad bowl.

Layer tomatoes, pickles, eggs, ham and onion over greens in bowl.

Spread dressing evenly over top of salad. Refrigerate.

Make-It-Easy Egg Salad

For the simplest egg salad ever, chop leftover hard-cooked eggs. Add chopped CLAUSSEN Pickles and KRAFT Mayo: Real or Light Mayonnaise. Stir gently to moisten.

Mediterranean Pasta Salad
(see recipe, page 112)

ON THE SIDE

Round out all your meals deliciously with this versatile collection of side dishes. Italian Pasta Salad, Spicy 20-Minute Potato Salad, Herb-Roasted Mediterranean Vegetables and the other salads, vegetables, pasta and rice dishes and breads are ideal counterparts to a wide variety of main dishes. And because they're so easy to assemble, it's a breeze to prepare one or two any night of the week.

Mediterranean Pasta Salad

(Photo on pages 110–111.)

Prep time: 20 minutes plus refrigerating

Makes 4 to 6 servings

2½ cups (6 ounces) rotini *or* bow tie pasta, cooked, drained

1 *each* medium zucchini and carrot, thinly sliced

1 *each* small green and red pepper, chopped

1 can (2¼ ounces) pitted ripe olives, drained

½ cup (2 ounces) ATHENOS Crumbled Feta Cheese

½ teaspoon crushed red pepper

1 cup prepared GOOD SEASONS Italian *or* Zesty Italian Salad Dressing

Mix all ingredients except salad dressing in large bowl. Toss to coat with dressing. Cover.

Refrigerate 1 hour or until ready to serve. Garnish with fresh mint, if desired.

Perfect Pasta

For pasta that's cooked just right, test it often near the end of the cooking time suggested on the package. The pasta is done when it's tender, but still slightly firm as you bite into it. To keep the pasta from cooking any further, immediately drain it in a colander.

Italian Pasta Salad

Prep time: 15 minutes plus refrigerating

Makes 8 servings

3 cups (8 ounces) rotini pasta, cooked, drained

2 cups broccoli flowerets

1 bottle (8 ounces) KRAFT House Italian with Olive Oil Blend Dressing

1 cup (4 ounces) KRAFT 100% Grated Parmesan Cheese

½ cup *each* chopped red pepper, pitted ripe olives and slivered red onion

Toss all ingredients. Refrigerate.

Garden *Tabbouleh*

Prep time: 25 minutes

Makes 10 servings

1	cup bulgur
1½	cups boiling water
¼	cup olive oil
2	to 3 tablespoons lemon juice
1	clove garlic, minced
½	teaspoon dried mint flakes
½	teaspoon salt
1	package (4 ounces) ATHENOS Crumbled Feta Cheese *or* Feta Cheese with Peppercorn
1	cup chopped fresh parsley
1	tomato, chopped
½	cup chopped green onions

Mix bulgur and boiling water; cover. Let stand 20 minutes or until bulgur is soft.

Stir in oil, juice, garlic, mint and salt.

Add remaining ingredients; mix lightly. Garnish with fresh mint leaves, if desired.

Lemon Juice Savvy

Freshly squeezed lemon juice gives a tantalizing citrus flavor to all types of dishes. To get the most juice, purchase a lemon that is heavy for its size. Before squeezing, leave the lemon at room temperature for 30 minutes. Then roll it under the palm of your hand a few times so more juice will flow. A medium lemon will yield about 3 tablespoons juice.

Lebanese Lentils & *Red Peppers*

Prep time: 10 minutes plus refrigerating   Cooking time: 30 minutes

Makes 6 to 8 servings

1 cup dry lentils
¾ cup chopped red pepper
⅓ cup chopped red onion
2 tablespoons chopped fresh mint (optional)
6 tablespoons olive oil
6 tablespoons balsamic vinegar
2 cloves garlic, minced
1 package (8 ounces) ATHENOS Feta Cheese, crumbled

Place lentils in saucepan. Pour enough water into pan to cover lentils by 2 inches. Cook on medium heat 30 minutes or until tender. Drain. Transfer to a bowl. Add red pepper, onion and mint. Refrigerate until ready to serve.

Mix oil, vinegar and garlic. Pour over lentil mixture; mix lightly.

Toss with cheese. Serve in red pepper quarters and garnish with additional fresh mint leaves, if desired.

Spicy *20-Minute* Potato Salad

Prep time: 5 minutes plus refrigerating   Cooking time: 14 minutes

Makes 6 servings

5 cups quartered small red potatoes

½ cup KRAFT Mayo Real Mayonnaise *or* MIRACLE WHIP Salad Dressing

⅛ to ¼ teaspoon *each* black pepper, ground red pepper and salt

⅓ cup *each* sliced celery and sliced green onions

Add potatoes to boiling water; cook 14 minutes or until fork-tender. Drain.

Mix mayo and seasonings in large bowl.

Add potatoes, celery and onions; mix lightly. Refrigerate.

Note: To use your microwave oven to cook the potatoes, place quartered potatoes and ⅓ cup water in 3-quart microwavable casserole; cover. Microwave on HIGH 14 to 16 minutes or until tender, stirring after 8 minutes. Drain.

Great American Potato Salad

Prep time: 20 minutes plus refrigerating

Makes 6 servings

¾ cup **MIRACLE WHIP** *or* **MIRACLE WHIP LIGHT Dressing**
1 teaspoon **prepared mustard**
¼ teaspoon **celery seed**
4 cups **cubed cooked potatoes (about 1½ pounds)**
½ cup *each* **sweet pickle relish and sliced celery**
Salt and pepper

Mix dressing, mustard and celery seed in large bowl.

Add potatoes, relish and celery; mix lightly. Season to taste with salt and pepper. Refrigerate. Garnish with celery leaves and sliced radishes.

Note: Red-skinned or new potatoes are recommended for this salad because they cube neatly after boiling and absorb the dressing readily.

Make-Ahead Salads

Prepare pasta or potato salads up to two days in advance by combining the KRAFT Mayo or MIRACLE WHIP with the seasonings and refrigerating this mixture separately from the cooked pasta or potatoes. Then, just before serving, stir the two together for a fresh, great-tasting salad.

Tomato & Orange Salad with Feta

Prep time: 15 minutes

Makes 8 servings

Dressing
- ¼ **cup olive oil**
- 1 **tablespoon balsamic vinegar**
- ¼ **teaspoon *each* salt and pepper**

Salad
- 4 **large tomatoes, sliced ¼ inch thick**
- 4 **oranges, peeled, sliced ¼ inch thick**
- 1 **package (8 ounces) ATHENOS Feta Cheese, sliced ⅛ inch thick**
- ⅔ **cup lightly packed small fresh basil leaves *or* 8 large fresh basil leaves, julienne-cut**

Mix oil, vinegar and seasonings for dressing.

Arrange tomatoes, oranges and cheese for salad alternately in overlapping circles on serving platter. Sprinkle with basil. Spoon dressing over salad.

Tomato Tips

The tomato is the rare fruit that actually is used as a vegetable. It enlivens savory salads, sauces and other dishes.
- When buying fresh tomatoes, look for plump, well-shaped fruit that is fairly firm-textured (but not hard), brightly colored and free of soft spots, bruises and cracks.
- If fresh tomatoes are a tad hard and need ripening, place them in a brown paper bag on the kitchen counter for a few days. When they are ripe and ready to eat, they will yield slightly to gentle pressure.

Mimosa Mold

Prep time: 15 minutes   Refrigerating time: 5½ hours

Makes 12 servings

1½ cups boiling water
  1 package (6 ounces) *or* 2 packages
     (3 ounces *each*) JELL-O Sparkling
     White Grape *or* **Sparkling Wild Berry**
     Flavor Gelatin Dessert
  2 cups cold seltzer *or* club soda
  1 can (11 ounces) mandarin orange
     segments, drained
  1 cup sliced strawberries

Stir boiling water into gelatin in large bowl at least 2 minutes until completely dissolved. Stir in cold seltzer. Refrigerate 1½ hours or until thickened. (Spoon drawn through leaves a definite impression.) Stir in oranges and strawberries. Spoon into 6-cup mold.

Refrigerate 4 hours or until firm. Unmold on lettuce-lined platter. Garnish with edible fresh flowers (tip, page 165). Store leftover gelatin mold in refrigerator.

Pear & Pecan Salad with Mixed Greens

Prep time: 15 minutes

Makes about 10 servings

1 **package (10 ounces) salad greens *or*
   6 cups torn leaf and romaine lettuce**
2 **medium pears, sliced**
1 **cup halved seedless red grapes**
1 **bottle (8 ounces) KRAFT Ranch Dressing
   or KRAFT FREE Ranch Fat Free Dressing**
⅓ **cup pecan *or* walnut halves, toasted
   KRAFT Blue Cheese Crumbles (optional)**

Toss greens, pears and grapes in large bowl.

Drizzle with dressing and top with pecans and cheese just before serving.

Spinach, Fruit & Feta Salad

Prep time: 15 minutes

Makes 6 servings

Dressing

- ¼ **cup olive oil**
- ¼ **cup fresh lemon juice***
- 2 **teaspoons honey**
- ¼ **teaspoon ground black pepper**

Salad

- 5 **cups torn spinach**
- 1 **cup *each* cantaloupe chunks and halved strawberries**
- 1 **cup (6 ounces) crumbled ATHENOS Feta Cheese**
- ½ **cup thinly sliced red onion cut into rings**
- ¼ **cup pitted ripe olives**

Mix oil, juice, honey and pepper for dressing in small bowl.

Toss spinach, fruit, cheese, onion and olives for salad in large bowl. Spoon dressing over spinach mixture.

***Note:** One large lemon, squeezed, will yield about ¼ cup fresh lemon juice.

Full-Flavored Feta Cheese

ATHENOS Feta Cheese adds a distinctively Mediterranean flavor to almost any dish. This robust cheese is delicious crumbled over a salad or pasta. Or, simply serve it with olives, bread and wine for a Mediterranean-style summer picnic.

Fresh Lettuce Salad with Bacon Vinaigrette

Prep time: 5 minutes   Cooking time: 10 minutes

Makes 8 servings

8	**cups torn mixed salad greens**
¼	**cup sliced green onions**
12	**slices OSCAR MAYER Center Cut Bacon, cut into 1-inch pieces**
¼	**cup vinegar**
½	**teaspoon salt**
⅛	**teaspoon pepper**
1	**teaspoon dill weed**

Place greens and onions in large serving bowl; set aside.

Cook bacon in large skillet on medium heat to desired crispness, stirring frequently. Drain bacon, reserving 2 tablespoons drippings in skillet. Place bacon on paper towels; set aside. Stir in vinegar, salt and pepper; bring to boil.

Pour dressing over greens mixture; toss. Add bacon and dill; toss lightly. Garnish with edible fresh flower (tip, page 165). Serve immediately.

Spicy Three Bean Salad

Prep time: 10 minutes plus refrigerating

Makes 8 servings

1   can (16 ounces) kidney beans, rinsed, drained

1   can (16 ounces) Great Northern beans, rinsed, drained

1   can (16 ounces) black beans, rinsed, drained

½   cup diced green pepper

½   cup diced red pepper

1   cup SEVEN SEAS VIVA Italian Dressing

Toss all ingredients in large bowl. Refrigerate. Serve in hollowed-out bell pepper halves, if desired.

Bruschetta Salad

Prep time: 10 minutes

Makes 6 servings

3   **cups tomato chunks**
1   **cup SEVEN SEAS VIVA Italian Dressing**
1   **cup slivered red onion**
1   **cup (4 ounces) KRAFT 100% Shredded Parmesan Cheese**
½   **pound day-old bread, cut into cubes**

Toss all ingredients. Garnish with fresh basil leaves. Serve immediately.

Time-Saving Products

For those evenings when mealtime is tight, why not take advantage of some of the high-quality convenience products on your supermarket shelves? You'll find:
• Packaged torn mixed salad greens
• OSCAR MAYER Meats
• LOUIS RICH CARVING BOARD Turkey or Ham
• Sliced chicken, pork and beef for stir-frying
• KRAFT Macaroni & Cheese Dinners
• TACO BELL HOME ORIGINALS Dinner Kits
• Canned tomato products with added seasonings
• MINUTE Rice
• SHAKE 'N BAKE Seasoned Coating Mixes
• KRAFT Shredded Cheeses
• DI GIORNO Pastas and Sauces
• TOMBSTONE Pizzas
• Frozen mashed potatoes
• JELL-O Instant Pudding & Pie Fillings

TACO BELL and HOME ORIGINALS are registered trademarks owned and licensed by Taco Bell Corp.

Classic *Caesar* Salad

Prep time: 5 minutes

Makes 4 main-dish servings or 8 side-salad servings

8 cups torn romaine lettuce *or*
   1 package (10 ounces) mixed *or*
   romaine salad greens
1 cup seasoned croutons
½ cup (2 ounces) KRAFT 100% Shredded
   or Grated Parmesan Cheese
¾ cup KRAFT Classic Caesar Dressing *or*
   KRAFT Caesar Italian Dressing

Toss lettuce, croutons and cheese in large salad bowl with dressing.

Serve with fresh lemon wedges and fresh ground pepper, if desired. Garnish with red onion flower and lemon slices.

Chicken Caesar Salad: Cook 1 pound boneless skinless chicken breasts, cut into strips, in additional ¼ cup dressing in skillet on medium heat about 8 minutes or until cooked through. Prepare salad as directed, arranging chicken over tossed salad.

Crisp, Clean Greens

White and apple cider vinegars can help keep greens and other vegetables at their peak. To clean greens, vegetables and fruits, wash them with a mixture of 2 to 3 tablespoons of vinegar per quart of water. To revive wilted greens, soak them in a quart of cold water and 1 tablespoon of vinegar.

Herb-Roasted Mediterranean Vegetables

Prep time: 15 minutes   Baking time: 40 minutes

Makes 6 to 8 servings

8   cups assorted vegetable pieces (such as cubed eggplant, zucchini and onion, halved carrots, cut-up peppers and baby turnips)
¼   cup olive oil
2   cloves garlic, minced
2   teaspoons dried rosemary leaves
1   teaspoon salt
½   cup (2 ounces) DI GIORNO Shredded Parmesan Cheese

Toss vegetables with oil, garlic, rosemary and salt. Place in 15×10×1-inch baking pan.

Bake at 375°F for 40 minutes or until vegetables are tender, stirring once or twice during cooking.

Sprinkle with cheese.

Grilled Vegetables

When you've purchased a basketful of vegetables at the farmer's market, grill them brushed with KRAFT Italian Dressing! Green peppers, onions, eggplant, zucchini, yellow squash, asparagus and mushrooms are all delicious hot off the grill. Plan on grilling vegetable slices or pieces 8 to 10 minutes or until cooked through, brushing frequently with dressing and turning occasionally.

Pasta with *Creamy Garlic* & Walnut Sauce

Prep time: 10 minutes   Cooking time: 15 minutes

Makes 6 servings

1½	**cups heavy cream**
1	**cup walnut halves, toasted, cooled**
¾	**cup (3 ounces) DI GIORNO Shredded Romano Cheese**
3	**cloves garlic, peeled**
1	**teaspoon salt**
½	**teaspoon ground black pepper**
1	**pound shaped pasta (such as medium bow ties)**

Place cream, walnuts, cheese, garlic, salt and pepper in food processor container fitted with steel blade; cover. Process until smooth.

Cook pasta as package directs; drain. Toss with sauce. Garnish with additional toasted walnuts and fresh herbs and serve immediately with additional cheese, if desired.

Manual Method: Finely grind cooled walnuts. Finely mince garlic. Mix cream, walnuts, cheese, garlic, salt and pepper. Continue as directed.

Toasting Nuts

Toasting gives nuts a deeper, richer flavor and helps them stay crisp when tossed in salads. Here's how to toast nuts: Spread them in a single layer in a shallow baking pan. Bake at 350°F for 5 to 10 minutes or until golden. Watch the nuts carefully and stir them once or twice so they don't burn.

Mediterranean Rice

Prep time: 5 minutes   Cooking time: 20 minutes

Makes 4 servings

3 tablespoons olive oil
⅓ cup finely chopped onion
1½ cups long grain rice, uncooked
1 can (13¾ ounces) chicken broth
¾ cup water
6 ounces ATHENOS Feta Cheese with
      Peppercorn, crumbled
2 tablespoons chopped fresh oregano *or*
      2 teaspoons dried oregano leaves

Heat oil in medium saucepan. Add onion; cook and stir 3 to 4 minutes or until tender. Add rice; cook and stir 1 minute.

Stir in broth and water. Bring to a boil. Reduce heat to low; cover. Simmer 15 minutes or until liquid is absorbed.

Stir in cheese and oregano. Garnish with fresh herbs, if desired.

Broccoli Rice Casserole

Prep time: 20 minutes   Baking time: 35 minutes

Makes 4 to 6 servings

½   **cup chopped onion**

2   **tablespoons butter *or* margarine, divided**

2   **cups hot cooked MINUTE Premium Long-Grain Rice**

1   **can (10¾ ounces) condensed cream of mushroom soup**

2   **cups fresh broccoli flowerets *or* 1 package (10 ounces) frozen chopped broccoli, cooked, well drained**

1   **jar (8 ounces) CHEEZ WHIZ Pasteurized Process Cheese Sauce**

½   **cup fresh bread cubes**

Cook and stir onion in 1 tablespoon of the butter in large skillet on medium heat until tender.

Add rice, soup, broccoli and process cheese sauce; mix lightly. Spoon into 1½-quart casserole. Toss remaining 1 tablespoon butter, melted, and bread cubes; sprinkle over casserole.

Bake at 350°F for 30 to 35 minutes or until thoroughly heated. Garnish with apple slices.

Garlicky Potatoes

Prep time: 5 minutes

Makes 4 servings

1   **envelope GOOD SEASONS Roasted Garlic *or* Italian Salad Dressing Mix**
4   **cups prepared mashed potatoes**

Stir salad dressing mix into potatoes. Serve immediately. Top with pat of butter, if desired. Serve with grilled or broiled steaks, chops, chicken or fish.

Quick & Easy *Risotto*
(Photo on page 155.)

Prep time: 10 minutes   Cooking time: 25 minutes

Makes 4 to 6 servings

2   **tablespoons olive oil**
1   **cup chopped mushrooms**
⅓   **cup sliced green onions**
1   **cup long grain rice, uncooked**
1½   **cups water**
½   **cup dry white wine**
¾   **cup (3 ounces) DI GIORNO Shredded Pecorino Romano Cheese, divided**
¼   **cup half-and-half *or* milk**

Heat oil in saucepan. Add mushrooms and onions; cook and stir on medium heat 5 minutes or until tender.

Stir in rice, water and wine. Bring to a boil. Reduce heat to low; cover. Simmer 20 minutes or until rice is tender.

Stir in ½ cup of the cheese and half-and-half. Serve with remaining cheese.

PARM PLUS!® *Breadsticks*

Prep time: 10 minutes   Baking time: 18 minutes

Makes 16

1   **can (11 ounces) refrigerated soft breadsticks**
3   **tablespoons melted butter *or* margarine**
½   **cup PARM PLUS! Seasoning Blend**

Separate and cut breadstick dough into 16 breadsticks.

Dip into butter; coat with seasoning blend. Twist; place on ungreased cookie sheet.

Bake at 350°F for 14 to 18 minutes or until golden brown.

Grilled Bread

(Photo on page 103.)

Prep time: 5 minutes   Grilling time: 6 minutes

Makes 12 servings

1   **bottle (8 ounces) KRAFT House Italian with Olive Oil Blend Dressing**
1   **loaf French bread, cut into slices**

Spread dressing generously over cut surfaces of bread. Place on grill over medium coals.

Grill 3 minutes on each side or until toasted. Serve with salads or grilled meats.

Bruschetta in a Breeze! Prepare as directed. Top grilled bread with chopped tomato and sliced green onions.

Italian Bread in an Instant! Cut bread in half lengthwise. Prepare as directed, placing bread, dressing-side down, on grill. Grill until toasted; top with sliced plum tomatoes, fresh basil and KRAFT Shredded Mozzarella Cheese. Place on grill, topped-side up; cover. Grill an additional 5 minutes.

A Super Sandwich! Cut bread in half lengthwise. Prepare as directed, placing bread, dressing-side down, on grill. Grill until toasted; top bread with OSCAR MAYER Sliced Meats, KRAFT Singles Process Cheese Food, lettuce and tomatoes.

Orange Oriental
Sesame Beef Stir-Fry
(recipe, page 144)

CASUAL GATHERINGS

G etting together with family and friends is as simple as a quick phone call and choosing from any of these extra quick recipes for informal gatherings. Dishes such as Perfect Pasta Pizza and Bistro Chicken with Parmesan are perfect for any occasion from a simple supper with the neighbors to an after-the-game victory celebration.

Orange *Oriental Sesame* Beef Stir-Fry

(Photo on pages 142–143.)

Prep time: 15 minutes   Cooking time: 10 minutes

Makes 4 servings

¼ **cup orange juice**
2 **tablespoons soy sauce**
1 **envelope GOOD SEASONS Oriental
   Sesame Salad Dressing Mix**
½ **cup oil**
1 **tablespoon grated orange peel**
1 **clove garlic, minced**
1 **pound lean boneless beef sirloin, cut
   into strips**
5 **cups assorted cut-up fresh vegetables
   or 1 package (16 ounces) frozen
   mixed vegetables, thawed
   Hot cooked rice**

Mix juice, soy sauce, salad dressing mix, oil, peel and garlic in cruet or small bowl as directed on envelope.

Heat 1 tablespoon of the dressing mixture in large skillet on medium heat. Add meat; cook and stir until cooked through. Add vegetables and remaining dressing mixture; cook and stir until vegetables are tender-crisp. Serve over rice.

Salad Dressing to the Rescue

Mix up your favorite GOOD SEASONS Salad Dressing Mix and keep some on hand to add a flavor boost to all types of foods. (It will store in the refrigerator for up to 4 weeks.) Use it as a dip for crusty bread or vegetables. Brush some on meats, seafood or chicken before grilling or roasting. Sauté vegetables or meats in the dressing for extra zing.

Casual Entertaining Made Easy

Although the word "entertaining" may conjure up images of hours spent in the kitchen, it doesn't have to be that way. Entertaining can be as unassuming as inviting friends over to kick off the weekend or asking the neighbors to stop by to celebrate a beautiful day.

The secret to casual entertaining is making it easy on yourself so that your guests—and you—can enjoy each other around good food. Here are a few tips to simplify any gathering:

• When choosing the menu, plan either all finger foods or go with a sit-down meal (it's easier to serve just one style).

• Build your menu around a simple, reliable main dish, such as one of the recipes in this section.

• Begin with only high-quality ingredients.

• Look to the produce aisle or salad bar of your supermarket for precut vegetables and ready-to-eat fruit. Then, artfully arrange them on pretty platters and serve with dips.

• Seek out a reliable bakery as a source of good bread. Served with Hot Bacon Cheese Spread (recipe, page 28), bread can become a speedy appetizer as well as complementing the main course.

• For dessert, consider a favorite high-quality ice cream or sorbet from your supermarket, or choose a dessert recipe that you can make ahead. That way, all you have to do at the last minute is brew coffee.

Meat Lover's Barbecued Steak

Prep time: 5 minutes   Grilling time: 20 minutes

Makes 4 to 6 servings

1½ **pounds beef steak, 1 inch thick**
1 **clove garlic, halved**
1 **large onion, cut into ¼-inch slices**
1 **cup KRAFT Original Barbecue Sauce or KRAFT THICK 'N SPICY Original Barbecue Sauce**

Rub both sides of steak with garlic clove halves.

Place steak and onion slices on greased grill over hot coals.

Grill, uncovered, 15 to 20 minutes or to desired doneness, brushing steak and onion slices frequently with barbecue sauce and turning occasionally.

Broiler Method: Prepare steak as directed, except place steak and onion slices on greased rack of broiler pan. Broil 15 to 20 minutes or to desired doneness, brushing steak and onion slices frequently with barbecue sauce and turning occasionally.

Improvise a Cooler

Having a big party? Use a kiddie swimming pool filled with ice as a large cooler. Set it alongside the buffet table to keep pitchers and cans of beverages well chilled. Or, if you have a large buffet table, put the ice-filled pool on your table and nestle bowls of salads in the ice.

Personalized Pasta Pizza
(recipe opposite page)

Perfect Pasta Pizza

Prep time: 15 minutes   Baking time: 25 minutes

Makes 4 servings

8   ounces spaghetti, cooked, drained
1   egg, beaten
¼   cup milk
¾   pound ground beef
1   can (14 ounces) tomato sauce
1   envelope GOOD SEASONS Garlic & Herb
      Salad Dressing Mix
1   cup KRAFT Shredded Low-Moisture
      Part-Skim Mozzarella Cheese

Toss spaghetti, egg and milk in large bowl. Spread evenly in greased 12-inch pizza pan.

Brown meat in medium skillet; drain. Stir in tomato sauce and salad dressing mix. Spoon over spaghetti crust. Sprinkle with cheese.

Bake at 350°F 20 to 25 minutes or until cheese is melted.

Personalized Pasta Pizza: Prepare pizza as directed, topping meat mixture with your favorite pizza toppings, such as pepperoni, mushrooms, olives and peppers; sprinkle with cheese. Bake as directed.

Perfect Pasta Pizza with Onion: Prepare pizza as directed, adding ½ cup chopped onion to meat when browning.

Steak & Spinach Salad

Prep time: 10 minutes plus marinating   Grilling or Broiling time: 20 minutes

Makes 4 servings

1	envelope GOOD SEASONS Gourmet Parmesan Italian Salad Dressing Mix
⅓	cup apple cider vinegar
⅓	cup olive oil
1	clove garlic, minced
1	beef sirloin steak, ½ to ¾ inch thick (1 pound)
8	cups torn spinach
1	cup sliced mushrooms
1	large tomato, cut into wedges
¼	cup sliced green onions

Mix salad dressing mix, vinegar, oil and garlic in cruet or small bowl as directed on envelope. Reserve ⅓ cup of the dressing mixture; refrigerate.

Pour remaining dressing over steak; cover. Refrigerate 1 hour to marinate. Drain; discard dressing mixture.

Place steak on greased grill over hot coals or on rack of broiler pan 2 to 3 inches from heat. Grill or broil 10 minutes on each side or to desired doneness. Cut into slices.

Toss spinach, mushrooms, tomato and onions with reserved ⅓ cup dressing mixture. Arrange steak slices over salad.

Chicken & Spinach Salad: Prepare as directed, substituting 1 pound boneless skinless chicken breasts for steak.

BBQ Bacon Cheeseburgers
(recipe opposite page)

Great American Potato
Salad (recipe, page 119)

BBQ Bacon *Cheeseburgers*

Prep time: 15 minutes   Grilling time: 12 minutes

Makes 4 sandwiches

1   **pound ground beef**
2   **tablespoons KRAFT Original Barbecue Sauce**
8   **KRAFT Deluxe Pasteurized Process American Cheese Slices**
4   **Kaiser *or* hamburger rolls, split, toasted**
    Lettuce
8   **slices OSCAR MAYER Bacon, crisply cooked**

Mix meat and barbecue sauce. Shape into 4 patties.

Place patties on grill over hot coals. Grill 8 to 12 minutes or to desired doneness, turning and brushing occasionally with additional barbecue sauce.

Top each patty with 2 process cheese slices. Continue grilling until process cheese is melted. Fill rolls with lettuce, cheeseburgers and bacon.

Quick Salad Serve-Alongs

For a fast side dish, dress up ready-to-use salad greens and your favorite salad dressing with pantry allies. Toss in canned whole kernel corn, black beans or garbanzo beans, crumbled tortilla chips, marinated artichoke hearts and/or hot or sweet roasted peppers. Or, team peanuts, walnuts or pecans with your favorite fruits, such as sliced apples or pears, grapes or sliced oranges, to add zip and color.

Herb-Roasted Lamb

Prep time: 5 minutes plus marinating   Baking time: 50 minutes plus standing

Makes 8 servings

1   **cup dry red wine**
1   **cup olive oil**
3   **cloves garlic, minced**
1   **tablespoon dried rosemary leaves**
2   **teaspoons dried thyme leaves**
1   **teaspoon** *each* **salt and pepper**
1   **butterflied leg of lamb (about
      3 pounds)**

Mix wine, oil, garlic and seasonings. Pour over lamb in large zipper-style plastic bag; seal bag. Marinate in refrigerator 2 hours or overnight, turning occasionally.

Place lamb on rack in roasting pan.

Bake at 350°F for 40 to 50 minutes or until meat thermometer reaches 160°F (medium). Let stand 10 minutes before slicing. Garnish with fresh rosemary.

Storing Olive Oil

Keep olive oil at its peak by storing it in a cool, dark place where it will last for up to a year. When used in a salad dressing that is chilled, the olive oil may solidify and the dressing may be too thick to pour immediately. This won't affect the flavor. Simply let the dressing stand at room temperature for 10 to 15 minutes, shake or mix it and serve.

Quick & Easy Risotto
(recipe, page 138)

Herb-Roasted Lamb
(recipe opposite page)

Thai Chicken and Sesame Noodles

Prep time: 10 minutes plus marinating   Cooking time: 15 minutes

Makes 4 servings

1   cup prepared **GOOD SEASONS** Oriental
    Sesame Salad Dressing, divided
1   **pound boneless skinless chicken breast**
    halves, cut into strips
2   **tablespoons** *each* **chunky peanut butter**
    and honey
½   **teaspoon crushed red pepper**
8   **ounces thin spaghetti, cooked, drained**
¾   **cup** *each* **shredded carrot and sliced**
    green onions
¼   **cup chopped cilantro**

Pour ⅓ cup of the dressing over chicken in medium bowl; toss to coat. Cover. Refrigerate 1 hour to marinate. Drain; discard dressing.

Mix remaining ⅔ cup dressing, peanut butter, honey and pepper; set aside.

Cook chicken in large skillet on medium-high heat about 8 minutes or until chicken is cooked through. Mix chicken, spaghetti, carrot, onions and cilantro in large bowl. Add peanut butter mixture; toss to coat. Garnish with cilantro sprig and carrot curls. Serve immediately.

Chopping Herbs

Make quick work of chopping fresh herbs. Just place the leaves in a glass measuring cup or a small bowl and cut them into tiny pieces with kitchen shears, using short, quick strokes.

Chicken Amandine

Prep time: 10 minutes   Cooking time: 12 minutes

Makes 4 servings

1   **envelope GOOD SEASONS Italian *or* Gourmet Parmesan Italian Salad Dressing Mix**
¾   **cup dry white wine *or* water**
¼   **cup olive oil**
1   **pound boneless skinless chicken breast halves**
½   **cup *each* sliced green onions and sliced almonds**

Mix salad dressing mix, wine and oil in cruet or small bowl as directed on envelope.

Heat ¼ cup of the dressing mixture in large skillet on medium heat. Add chicken; cook 8 minutes or until cooked through and browned on both sides.

Add remaining dressing mixture, onions and almonds. Cook 4 minutes, stirring constantly. Serve over hot cooked rice, if desired. Garnish with sliced green onion.

Marinated *Shish Kabobs*

Prep time: 15 minutes plus marinating   Grilling time: 14 minutes

Makes 6 servings

¾   cup **KRAFT Italian Dressing**

1¼   **pounds boneless skinless chicken breasts *or* beef tenderloin, cut into 1½-inch chunks**

2   **cups assorted vegetables (such as pepper chunks, zucchini slices and onion wedges)**

Pour dressing over chicken and vegetables in large zipper-style plastic bag; seal bag. Marinate in refrigerator 2 hours or overnight, turning occasionally.

Thread chicken and vegetables on 6 skewers.

Grill over medium coals 5 to 7 minutes on each side or until cooked through. Serve with couscous, if desired. Garnish with fresh herbs.

Note: If using wooden skewers, soak them in water 30 minutes before using.

Bistro Chicken with Parmesan

Prep time: 25 minutes

Makes 4 servings

2 boneless skinless chicken breast halves, grilled *or* broiled, cut into ¼-inch slices

2 cups cooked penne *or* rotini pasta

1 cup quartered cherry tomatoes

1 cup DI GIORNO Shredded Parmesan Cheese

½ cup prepared GOOD SEASONS Gourmet Caesar *or* Italian Salad Dressing

⅓ cup lightly packed fresh basil leaves, cut into strips

¼ cup *each* chopped red onion and sun-dried tomatoes, drained, chopped

Mix all ingredients. Serve warm or chilled. Garnish with fresh basil.

Turkey and *Basil* Cream Sauce

Prep time: 5 minutes   Cooking time: 11 minutes

Makes 4 servings

1   **pound LOUIS RICH Breast of Turkey, cut into ¼-inch-thick slices**
¼   **cup water**
½   **cup *each* KRAFT Mayo Real Mayonnaise and milk**
¼   **teaspoon dried basil leaves**
1   **small tomato, chopped**
1   **green onion, sliced**

Place turkey and water in skillet; cover. Heat on medium heat 5 to 7 minutes. Drain.

Heat and stir mayo, milk and basil in small saucepan on medium heat 4 minutes or until smooth and slightly thickened. Serve sauce over turkey; sprinkle with tomato and onion. Garnish with fresh basil.

Margarita *Shrimp and Vegetable* Kabobs

Prep time: 20 minutes plus marinating   Grilling time: 15 minutes

Makes 4 servings

1   envelope GOOD SEASONS Italian Salad Dressing Mix
½   cup oil
¼   cup tequila
¼   cup lime juice
1   pound large shrimp (21 to 30), cleaned
   Assorted cut-up fresh vegetables, such as peppers, onions, zucchini and mushrooms

Mix salad dressing mix, oil, tequila and lime juice until well blended. Pour over shrimp and vegetables; cover. Refrigerate 1 hour or overnight to marinate. Drain.

Arrange shrimp and vegetables on skewers.

Grill kabobs on grill over medium-hot coals 10 to 15 minutes, turning once. Garnish with lime slices and edible fresh flower (tip, page 165).

Shrimp with *Tomato & Feta*

Prep time: 20 minutes   Cooking time: 12 minutes

Makes 4 servings

2 tablespoons olive oil
½ cup chopped onion
1 can (28 ounces) Italian-style plum
    tomatoes, drained, cut up
⅓ cup dry white wine
2 teaspoons dried oregano leaves
12 ounces medium shrimp, cleaned
1 package (4 ounces) ATHENOS Crumbled
    Feta Cheese
2 tablespoons chopped fresh parsley

Heat oil in large skillet. Add onion; cook and stir on medium heat 3 minutes. Add tomatoes, wine and oregano. Bring to a boil. Reduce heat to low; simmer, uncovered, 5 minutes or until thickened.

Add shrimp. Cook 3 minutes, stirring frequently, until shrimp are pink.

Sprinkle with cheese; simmer 1 minute. Stir in parsley. Serve with hot cooked rice, if desired. Garnish with fresh herbs.

Savory *Feta-Filled* Shells

Prep time: 20 minutes   Baking time: 20 minutes

Makes 4 servings

1   package (10 ounces) frozen chopped
      spinach, thawed, well drained *or*
      1 package (10 ounces) fresh spinach,
      stems removed, cooked, well drained
1   cup ricotta cheese
1   package (8 ounces) ATHENOS Feta
      Cheese, crumbled, divided
¼   teaspoon garlic powder
12 jumbo macaroni shells, cooked,
      drained
1½ cups marinara sauce

Mix spinach, ricotta cheese, 6 ounces of the feta cheese and garlic powder.

Fill shells with spinach mixture. Place in 2-quart square or rectangular baking dish. Pour sauce over shells. Top with remaining 2 ounces feta cheese.

Bake at 350°F for 20 minutes. Serve with mixed green salad, if desired. Garnish with fresh herbs.

Edible Flowers

Add a splash of color to dishes with edible flowers. Favorite edible flowers include the rose, viola, pansy, calendula, chamomile, carnation, nasturtium, violet, bachelor's button and geranium blossom (not leaf). Make sure the flowers are nontoxic and free of chemicals. If you have any doubt about whether a flower's blossom, stem or leaf is edible, check with a reliable source.

Coconut Sweet
Potato Casserole
(recipe, page 169)

Roast Turkey with
STOVE TOP® Stuffing
(recipe, page 168)

Spiced Cranberry
Orange Mold
(recipe, page 170)

Classic Green
Bean Casserole
(recipe, page 169)

CELEBRATION MENUS

W hatever the occasion—

Christmas, a birthday or a family

reunion—food plays an important part

in the festivities. Count on these menus,

filled with quick-to-fix and make-ahead

ideas, for your inspiration. After all, the

Kraft Kitchens have been helping

families celebrate special days with

memorable foods for generations.

Roast Turkey with
STOVE TOP® Stuffing

(Photo on pages 166–167.)

ready-to-cook weight	oven temperature	roasting time
8 to 12 pounds	325°F	3 to 3½ hours
12 to 14 pounds	325°F	3½ to 4 hours
14 to 18 pounds	325°F	4 to 4¼ hours
18 to 20 pounds	325°F	4¼ to 4¾ hours
20 to 24 pounds	325°F	4¾ to 5¼ hours

TO STUFF THE TURKEY, spoon some stuffing loosely into neck cavity. Pull the neck skin over stuffing; fasten to back with a short skewer. Loosely spoon stuffing into the body cavity; do not pack. (Do not use more than ¾ cup stuffing per pound of turkey.) Spoon any remaining stuffing into a casserole; cover. Refrigerate until ready to bake. Tuck the drumsticks under the band of skin that crosses the tail. (If there isn't a band, tie drumsticks to tail.) Twist the wing tips under back.

PLACE TURKEY, breast side up, on a rack in a shallow pan. If desired, brush with cooking oil. Place a meat thermometer in the center of an inside thigh muscle, not touching bone. Cover loosely with foil. Press foil over drumsticks and neck. Roast in a 325°F oven, using timings above as a guide.

DURING ROASTING, baste with drippings occasionally, if desired. When bird is ⅔ done, cut skin or string between drumsticks. Remove foil the last 30 to 45 minutes. When done, thigh meat should be 180°F and the stuffing should be at least 165°F. (Check temperature of stuffing with a meat thermometer, preferably an instant-read type. If you don't have an accurate thermometer, consider baking the stuffing in a covered casserole alongside the bird.) The temperatures will rise on standing. The meat should be tender and the juices from the thigh should run clear. Remove the turkey from oven; cover loosely with foil. Let stand 20 minutes before carving.

Holiday Feast

Roast Turkey with STOVE TOP® Stuffing
Coconut Sweet Potato Casserole
Classic Green Bean Casserole
Spiced Cranberry Orange Mold
Double Decker Pie

Coconut Sweet Potato Casserole

(Photo on pages 166–167.)

Prep time: 20 minutes   Baking time: 50 minutes

Makes 8 servings

1   **can (40 ounces) sweet potatoes, drained, cut up**
1   **apple, peeled, thinly sliced**
½   **cup maple-flavored syrup**
2   **tablespoons butter *or* margarine, melted**
½   **cup BAKER'S ANGEL FLAKE Coconut**

Place sweet potatoes in greased 9-inch square baking dish; top with apple slices.

Mix syrup and butter; pour over apple. Sprinkle with coconut; cover.

Bake at 350°F for 30 minutes. Uncover. Bake an additional 20 minutes or until apple is tender and coconut is lightly browned.

Classic Green Bean Casserole

(Photo on pages 166–167.)

Prep time: 5 minutes   Baking time: 35 minutes

Makes 8 servings

3   **packages (9 ounces *each*) frozen French cut green beans, thawed, drained**
1   **can (10¾ ounces) condensed cream of mushroom soup**
1   **jar (8 ounces) CHEEZ WHIZ Pasteurized Process Cheese Sauce *or* 1 cup CHEEZ WHIZ LIGHT Pasteurized Process Cheese Product**
⅛   **teaspoon pepper**
1   **can (2.8 ounces) French fried onions, divided**

Mix all ingredients except ½ can onions in 1½-quart casserole.

Bake at 350°F for 30 minutes. Top with remaining ½ can onions. Bake an additional 5 minutes.

Spiced *Cranberry* Orange Mold

(Photo on pages 166–167.)

Prep time: 15 minutes   Refrigerating time: 5½ hours

Makes 10 servings

1½ **cups boiling water**
 1 **package (6 ounces) *or* 2 packages (3 ounces *each*) JELL-O Cranberry Flavor Gelatin Dessert**
 ½ **teaspoon ground cinnamon**
 1 **can (16 ounces) whole berry cranberry sauce**
 1 **cup cold water**
 1 **orange, sectioned, diced**
 ½ **cup chopped walnuts, toasted**

Stir boiling water into gelatin and cinnamon in large bowl at least 2 minutes until completely dissolved. Stir in cranberry sauce until melted. Stir in cold water. Refrigerate about 1½ hours or until thickened. (Spoon drawn through leaves a definite impression.)

Stir in orange and walnuts. Spoon into 5-cup mold.

Refrigerate 4 hours or until firm. Unmold. Garnish as desired. Store leftover gelatin mold in refrigerator.

POST® GRAPE-NUTS® *Low Fat* Crust

Prep time: 10 minutes   Baking time: 5 minutes

Makes 1 (9-inch) crust

 1 **cup POST GRAPE-NUTS Cereal**
 ¼ **cup frozen apple juice concentrate, thawed**

Place cereal in food processor container fitted with steel blade; cover. Process until finely crushed. Mix cereal crumbs and thawed apple juice concentrate in small bowl until well blended. Press onto bottom and up side of 9-inch pie plate.

Bake at 350°F for 5 minutes or until light golden brown. Cool on wire rack.

Double Decker Pie

Prep time: 10 minutes   Refrigerating time: 4 hours

Makes 8 servings

2   cups cold skim milk, divided
1   package (4-serving size) JELL-O Chocolate Flavor Fat Free Instant Pudding & Pie Filling
1   tub (8 ounces) COOL WHIP LITE Whipped Topping, thawed, divided
1   POST® GRAPE-NUTS® Low Fat Crust (recipe opposite page)
1   package (4-serving size) JELL-O Vanilla Flavor Fat Free Instant Pudding & Pie Filling

Pour 1 cup of the milk into medium bowl. Add chocolate flavor pudding mix. Beat with wire whisk 1 minute. (Mixture will be thick.) Gently stir in ½ of the whipped topping. Spoon evenly into crust.

Pour remaining 1 cup milk into another medium bowl. Add vanilla flavor pudding mix. Beat with wire whisk 1 minute. (Mixture will be thick.) Gently stir in remaining whipped topping. Spread over pudding layer in crust.

Refrigerate 4 hours or until set. Garnish with additional whipped topping and candy pieces. Store leftover pie in refrigerator.

Spiced Brazilian
Chocolate
(recipe, page 174)

Multi-Grain Scones
(recipe, page 173) and
Citrus Muffins (recipe,
page 175)

Cheese omelet

Easy Potato Bake
(recipe, page 174)

Multi-Grain Scones

Prep time: 20 minutes   Baking time: 14 minutes

Makes 16

2 cups flour
¼ cup sugar
2 teaspoons CALUMET Baking Powder
¼ teaspoon salt
½ cup (1 stick) butter *or* margarine, chilled
1 cup POST MORNING TRADITIONS GREAT GRAINS Whole Grain Cereal, any variety
3 eggs, divided
⅓ cup heavy cream
2 tablespoons water

Mix flour, sugar, baking powder and salt in large bowl. Cut in butter until mixture resembles coarse crumbs. Stir in cereal. Beat 2 of the eggs in small bowl; stir in cream. Add to flour mixture; stir until soft dough forms. Shape into ball.

Knead dough on lightly floured surface until smooth. Roll to 12×6-inch rectangle. Cut into 8 (3-inch) squares; cut each square in half diagonally. Place on lightly greased cookie sheet. Beat remaining egg and water; brush over tops.

Bake at 425°F for 12 to 14 minutes or until lightly browned. Serve warm.

Special Occasion Brunch

Cheese omelet (use your favorite recipe)
Easy Potato Bake
Fresh fruit plate
Multi-Grain Scones or Citrus Muffins
Spiced Brazilian Chocolate

Easy Potato Bake

(Photo on page 172.)

Prep time: 10 minutes   Baking time: 1 hour

Makes 12 to 16 servings

1 **package (32 ounces) frozen Southern-style hash brown potatoes**
2 **cups BREAKSTONE'S *or* KNUDSEN Sour Cream**
2 **cups KRAFT Shredded Cheddar Cheese**
1 **can (10¾ ounces) condensed cream of chicken soup**
1 **cup *each* chopped green onions and corn flake crumbs**
2 **tablespoons butter *or* margarine, melted**

Mix potatoes, sour cream, cheese, soup and onions.

Spoon into greased 13×9-inch baking dish. Toss crumbs and butter; sprinkle over potato mixture.

Bake at 375°F for 1 hour.

Spiced *Brazilian* Chocolate

(Photo on page 172.)

Prep time: 10 minutes   Cooking time: 10 minutes

Makes 7 servings

1 **square BAKER'S Unsweetened Baking Chocolate, chopped**
2 **cups freshly brewed MAXWELL HOUSE Coffee, any variety**
¼ **cup sugar**
1 **teaspoon ground cinnamon**
1½ **cups milk**
1½ **teaspoons vanilla**

Heat chocolate and coffee in heavy saucepan on very low heat, stirring constantly with wire whisk until chocolate is melted and mixture is smooth.

Stir in sugar and cinnamon. Bring to boil. Stir until sugar is dissolved. Gradually stir in milk and vanilla. Stirring occasionally, heat thoroughly. Serve with whipped cream and orange peel or additional ground cinnamon, if desired.

Citrus Muffins

(Photo on page 172.)

Prep time: 15 minutes   Baking time: 20 minutes

Makes 12

1⅓   **cups flour**
½   **cup sugar**
1   **tablespoon CALUMET Baking Powder**
¼   **teaspoon salt**
1   **egg**
1   **cup milk**
⅓   **cup butter** *or* **margarine, melted**
1½   **teaspoons grated orange peel**
1½   **cups POST GREAT GRAINS Whole Grain Cereal**

Mix flour, sugar, baking powder and salt in large bowl. Beat egg in small bowl; stir in milk, butter and orange peel. Add to flour mixture; stir just until moistened. (Batter will be lumpy.) Stir in cereal.

Spoon batter into greased or paper-lined muffin pan, filling each cup ⅔ full.

Bake at 400°F for 20 minutes or until golden brown. Serve warm.

Notes: Add ⅓ cup raisins or dried blueberries, if desired.

   Recipe makes 24 to 30 miniature muffins. Spray pan with no stick cooking spray. Bake 15 minutes.

Party Preparation

Planning is critical for any special get-together. Here are a few tips to help you get organized ahead of time.
• Set your table a day or two prior to the party.
• Label all serving dishes and utensils. Cover everything with a sheet to keep off the dust.
• Write a preparation schedule. It will ensure that all the food will be ready on time.
• Cut down on your preparation time by asking each guest to bring a favorite dish.

Easy Wrap Sandwiches
(recipe opposite page)

Crunchy Bacon Coleslaw
(recipe, page 178)

Easy Wrap Sandwiches

Flour tortilla
KRAFT Mayo Real Mayonnaise *or*
 MIRACLE WHIP Salad Dressing
Lettuce
CLAUSSEN Kosher Dill Sandwich Slices
KRAFT Singles Process Cheese Food
OSCAR MAYER Smoked Cooked Ham

Spread tortilla with mayo.

Top with lettuce, pickles, process cheese food and ham. Fold up sides of tortilla to center, slightly overlapping. Secure with garnished toothpick, if desired.

Easy Wrap Sandwich with Turkey:
Substitute LOUIS RICH Oven Roasted Turkey Breast for ham and TACO BELL HOME ORIGINALS Thick 'N Chunky Salsa for pickles.

TACO BELL and HOME ORIGINALS are registered trademarks owned and licensed by Taco Bell Corp.

Family Reunion Picnic

Caesar Dip
Easy Wrap Sandwiches
Crunchy Bacon Coleslaw
Baked beans (use your favorite recipe)
PHILADELPHIA® Cheesecake

Crunchy Bacon Coleslaw

(Photo on page 176.)

Prep time: 15 minutes plus refrigerating

Makes 10 servings or about 4 cups

¾ cup **MIRACLE WHIP** *or* **MIRACLE WHIP LIGHT Dressing**
1 tablespoon sugar
1½ teaspoons cider vinegar
4 cups shredded green cabbage
1 cup shredded red cabbage
½ cup chopped peanuts
4 slices **OSCAR MAYER Bacon, crisply cooked, crumbled**

Mix dressing, sugar and vinegar in large bowl.

Add remaining ingredients; mix lightly. Refrigerate. Serve in lettuce-lined bowl.

Quick Crunchy Bacon Coleslaw:
Prepare as directed, substituting 1 package (8 ounces) coleslaw blend for shredded green and red cabbage. Substitute 1 can (3 ounces) OSCAR MAYER Real Bacon Bits for bacon slices.

Crunchy Carrot Bacon Coleslaw:
Prepare as directed, adding ¼ cup shredded carrot.

Buying Cabbage

When purchasing cabbage for coleslaw, feel the weight of a cabbage in the palm of your hand. It should be firm and heavy for its size. Look for healthy, bright leaves free from withering or brown spots. Keep in mind that a 1-pound head will yield about 4 cups of shredded cabbage.

Caesar Dip

Prep time: 10 minutes

Makes 2 cups

1   **package (8 ounces) PHILADELPHIA Cream Cheese, softened**

1   **cup (4 ounces) KRAFT 100% Grated Parmesan Cheese**

½   **cup KRAFT Classic Caesar Dressing**

1   **cup chopped romaine lettuce**

½   **cup croutons**

Beat cream cheese, Parmesan cheese and dressing with electric mixer on medium speed until well blended.

Spread on bottom of 9-inch pie plate. Top with lettuce and croutons. Sprinkle with additional Parmesan cheese, if desired. Garnish with lemon wedges. Serve with crackers.

PHILADELPHIA® *Cheesecake*

Prep time: 10 minutes plus refrigerating

Makes 8 servings

1   package (8 ounces) PHILADELPHIA Cream Cheese, softened
⅓   cup sugar
1   tub (8 ounces) COOL WHIP Whipped Topping, thawed
1   prepared graham cracker crumb crust (6 ounces *or* 9 inches)*

Mix cream cheese and sugar with electric mixer on medium speed until well blended. Gently stir in whipped topping.

Spoon into crust. Refrigerate 3 hours or overnight. Top with fresh fruit or cherry pie filling, if desired.

*Note: To transfer a purchased crust to your own pie plate, use kitchen shears to carefully cut foil pan. Then, peel pan from crust and place in pie plate.

Make-Ahead Cheesecake

Simplify last-minute preparations by making PHILADELPHIA® Cheesecake ahead of time and freezing it until needed. Before your party, place the frozen cheesecake in the refrigerator to thaw for about 8 hours.

Rocky Road Chocolate Silk Pie

Prep time: 20 minutes plus refrigerating

Makes 8 servings

1   **package (9.2 ounces) JELL-O No Bake Chocolate Silk Pie**
⅓   **cup butter *or* margarine, melted**
1⅔   **cups cold milk**
1   **cup miniature marshmallows**
½   **cup chopped nuts**

Mix Crumbs and butter thoroughly with fork in 9-inch pie plate until crumbs are well moistened. Press firmly against sides of pie plate first, using finger or large spoon to shape edge. Press remaining crumbs firmly onto bottom using measuring cup.

Beat cold milk and Filling Mix with electric mixer on low speed until blended. Beat on medium speed 3 minutes. (Filling will be thick.) Stir in marshmallows and nuts. Spoon into crust.

Refrigerate at least 1 hour. Top with thawed COOL WHIP Whipped Topping and decorative candy sprinkles, if desired. Store leftover pie in refrigerator.

Birthday Dinner

Peach-Glazed Pork Chops
Roasted Italian Potatoes
Steamed sugarsnap peas (use your favorite recipe)
Rocky Road Chocolate Silk Pie
GENERAL FOODS INTERNATIONAL COFFEES
Italian Cappuccino or Suisse Mocha Flavor

Peach-Glazed Pork Chops

Prep time: 15 minutes   Baking time: 40 minutes

Makes 6 servings

1   can (8½ ounces) peach slices,
     undrained
     Hot water
1   package (6 ounces) STOVE TOP Stuffing
     Mix for Pork
¼   cup (½ stick) butter *or* margarine, cut
     into pieces
6   pork chops, ½ inch thick
⅓   cup peach *or* apricot preserves
1   tablespoon Dijon mustard

Drain peaches, reserving syrup. Add hot water to syrup to measure 1½ cups. Mix syrup mixture, contents of Vegetable/Seasoning Packet and butter in large bowl until butter is melted. Stir in Stuffing Crumbs and peaches. Let stand 5 minutes.

Spoon stuffing into 13×9-inch baking pan. Arrange chops over stuffing. Mix preserves and mustard. Spoon over chops.

Bake at 375°F for 40 minutes or until chops are cooked through.

Roasted Italian Potatoes

Prep time: 10 minutes   Baking time: 45 minutes

Makes 6 to 8 servings

2   pounds potatoes, cut into quarters
½   cup KRAFT Zesty Italian Dressing
½   cup (2 ounces) KRAFT 100% Grated
     Parmesan Cheese

Toss potatoes with dressing and cheese. Place in 13×9-inch baking pan.

Bake at 400°F for 40 to 45 minutes or until lightly browned.

Spinach & Orange Salad

Prep time: 10 minutes

Makes 6 servings

8 cups torn spinach

1½ cups fresh orange sections *or* 2 cans (11 ounces *each*) mandarin orange segments, drained

1 package (4 ounces) ATHENOS Crumbled Feta Cheese

½ cup sliced red onion

⅓ cup sliced almonds

1 envelope GOOD SEASONS Italian *or* Oriental Sesame Salad Dressing Mix

Toss spinach, oranges, cheese, onion and almonds in large bowl.

Prepare salad dressing mix as directed on envelope. Toss with salad. Garnish with edible fresh flowers (tip, page 165).

PARM PLUS!® *Potatoes*

Prep time: 10 minutes   Baking time: 45 minutes

Makes 8 servings

2 pounds new potatoes, cut into quarters

⅓ cup olive oil

1 cup (4 ounces) PARM PLUS! Seasoning Blend

Toss potatoes with oil. Add seasoning blend; mix lightly. Place in 15×10×1-inch baking pan.

Bake at 400°F for 45 minutes.

Easter Dinner

Baked ham (use your favorite recipe)
Spinach & Orange Salad
PARM PLUS!® Potatoes
Sparkling White Grape Sorbet (recipe, page 228)

Creamy Lemon Pie
(recipe, page 191)

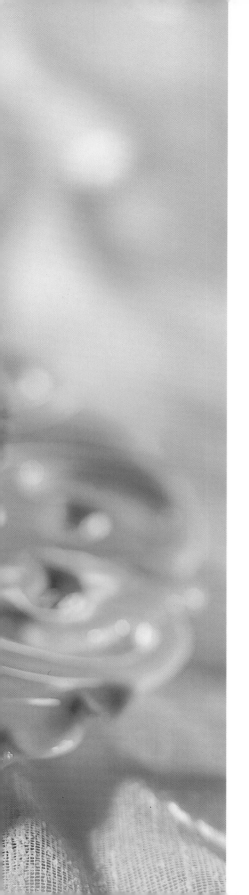

BEST-LOVED DESSERTS

For an after-dinner finale, late-evening coffee with friends or the perfect treat for a child's party, this chapter is filled with recipes for irresistible, yet simple to make, desserts. Whether you choose Cranberry Pear Crisp, Easy Mocha Cheesecake, Almond Macaroon Brownies or one of the other luscious choices, you'll agree that sweet dreams begin here.

Coffee Cheesecake Pie

Prep time: 20 minutes plus refrigerating   Baking time: 40 minutes plus cooling

Makes 8 servings

2 packages (8 ounces *each*) PHILADELPHIA
   Cream Cheese, softened*
½ cup sugar
2 eggs
⅓ cup freshly brewed double strength
   MAXWELL HOUSE Italian Espresso Roast
   Coffee, at room temperature
1 ready-to-use chocolate flavor crumb
   crust (6 ounces *or* 9 inches)
1 square BAKER'S Semi-Sweet Baking
   Chocolate, melted
   Coffee Caramel Sauce (recipe follows)

Mix cream cheese and sugar in large bowl with electric mixer on medium speed until well blended. Add eggs and coffee; mix until blended.

Pour into crust.

Bake at 350°F for 35 to 40 minutes or until center is almost set. Cool completely on wire rack.

Refrigerate at least 3 hours or overnight. Drizzle chocolate over top of pie.

Serve with Coffee Caramel Sauce. Garnish with fresh raspberries and chocolate leaves (tip, page 214). Store leftover pie in refrigerator.

*Note: To soften cream cheese, microwave on HIGH 20 to 30 seconds.

Coffee Caramel Sauce: Heat 1 cup KRAFT Caramel Topping and 2 tablespoons freshly brewed strong MAXWELL HOUSE Italian Espresso Roast Coffee in small saucepan on low heat, stirring constantly until well mixed and warm. Store leftover sauce in refrigerator. Makes 1 cup.

Coffee Cheesecake Pie
(recipe opposite page)

Creamy *Lemon* Pie

(Photo on pages 188–189.)

Prep time: 15 minutes   Refrigerating time: 4 hours

Makes 8 servings

1¾   **cups cold milk**

2   **packages (4-serving size *each*) JELL-O Vanilla Flavor Instant Pudding & Pie Filling**

1   **can (6 ounces) frozen lemonade concentrate, thawed**

1   **tub (8 ounces) COOL WHIP Whipped Topping, thawed**

1   **prepared graham cracker crumb crust (6 ounces *or* 9 inches)**

Pour milk into large bowl. Add pudding mixes. Beat with wire whisk 30 seconds. Add concentrate. Beat with wire whisk 30 seconds. (Mixture will be thick.) Immediately stir in whipped topping. Spoon into crust.

Refrigerate 4 hours or until set. Garnish with lemon slices. Store leftover pie in refrigerator.

White Chocolate *Cheesecake*

Prep time: 20 minutes plus refrigerating

Makes 8 servings

1   **package (11.1 ounces) JELL-O No Bake Real Cheesecake**

2   **tablespoons sugar**

⅓   **cup butter *or* margarine, melted**

1½   **cups cold milk**

1   **package (6 squares) BAKER'S Premium White Baking Chocolate Squares, melted**

Mix Crumbs, sugar and butter thoroughly with fork in 9-inch pie plate until crumbs are well moistened. Press firmly against sides of pie plate first, using fingers or large spoon to shape edge. Press remaining crumbs firmly onto bottom of pie plate, using measuring cup.

Beat cold milk and Filling Mix with electric mixer on low speed until blended. Beat on medium speed 3 minutes. (Filling will be thick.) Stir in melted white chocolate. Spoon into crust.

Refrigerate at least 1 hour. Garnish with Pastel Marble Flowers (tip below). Store leftover cheesecake in refrigerator.

Pastel Marble Flowers

Put 2 packages (6 ounces *each*) BAKER'S Premium White Baking Chocolate Squares in separate medium microwavable bowls. Microwave on HIGH 2 minutes or until white chocolates are almost melted, stirring halfway through heating time. Stir until white chocolates are completely melted.

Stir 3 to 5 drops red food coloring into 1 bowl of white chocolate, keeping second bowl of chocolate white. Alternately spoon tinted and plain white chocolates onto wax paper-lined cookie sheet. Tap cookie sheet on table top to evenly disperse chocolate. Swirl white chocolates with knife several times for marbled effect. Refrigerate 1 hour or until firm. Use vegetable peeler to shave off pieces. Shape pieces into flowers.

PHILADELPHIA 3-STEP®
Strawberry Layer Cheesecake

Prep time: 10 minutes   Baking time: 40 minutes

Makes 8 servings

2 packages (8 ounces *each*) PHILADELPHIA Cream Cheese, softened
½ cup sugar
½ teaspoon vanilla
2 eggs
¼ cup KRAFT Strawberry Preserves
5 drops red food coloring
1 ready-to-use graham cracker crumb crust (6 ounces *or* 9 inches)

Mix cream cheese, sugar and vanilla with electric mixer on medium speed until well blended. Add eggs; mix until blended. Stir preserves and food coloring into 1 cup of the batter.

Pour strawberry batter over crust. Top with remaining plain batter.

Bake at 350°F for 40 minutes or until center is almost set. Cool. Refrigerate 3 hours or overnight. Garnish with thawed COOL WHIP Whipped Topping and fresh strawberries.

Use a Springform Pan

If you have a springform pan, it's easy to adapt the PHILADELPHIA 3-STEP® Strawberry Layer Cheesecake to use it. Mix 1½ cups graham cracker crumbs, 3 tablespoons sugar and ⅓ cup butter *or* margarine, melted; press onto bottom of 9-inch springform pan. Double ingredients in recipe for batter. Mix and layer over crust as directed. Bake at 350°F for 55 minutes or until center is almost set. Loosen cake from rim of pan; cool before removing rim of pan. Makes 12 servings.

Easy *Mocha* Cheesecake

Prep time: 15 minutes   Refrigerating time: 1 hour

Makes 8 servings

1   **package (11.1 ounces) JELL-O No Bake
    Real Cheesecake**
⅓   **cup butter *or* margarine, melted**
2   **tablespoons sugar**
1½ **cups cold milk**
1   **envelope (15 grams) GENERAL FOODS
    INTERNATIONAL COFFEES, Suisse Mocha
    Flavor, French Vanilla Cafe Flavor *or*
    Irish Cream Cafe Flavor**

Mix Crumbs, butter and sugar thoroughly with fork in 9-inch pie plate until crumbs are well moistened. Press firmly against side of pie plate first, using finger or large spoon to shape edge. Press remaining crumbs firmly onto bottom of pie plate, using measuring cup.

Beat milk, flavored instant coffee and Filling Mix in large bowl with electric mixer on low speed until blended. Beat on medium speed 3 minutes. (Filling will be thick.) Spoon into crust.

Refrigerate at least 1 hour. Garnish with white and dark chocolate sticks (tip below) and candies. Store leftover cheesecake in refrigerator.

Chocolate Sticks

To make white or dark chocolate sticks to decorate desserts, melt a square of BAKER'S Semi-Sweet Baking Chocolate or Premium White Baking Chocolate. Brush in a 2-inch strip onto clear plastic wrap. Pleat so chocolate wrinkles. Refrigerate until firm. To make sticks, simply pull the plastic wrap flat so the firm chocolate breaks into sticks.

PHILADELPHIA 3-STEP®
Double Layer Pumpkin Cheesecake

Prep time: 10 minutes   Baking time: 40 minutes plus cooling   Refrigerating time: 3 hours

Makes 8 servings

2 packages (8 ounces *each*) **PHILADELPHIA Cream Cheese, softened**
½ cup sugar
½ teaspoon vanilla
2 eggs
½ cup canned pumpkin
½ teaspoon ground cinnamon
  Dash *each* ground cloves and nutmeg
1 ready-to-use graham cracker crumb crust (6 ounces *or* 9 inches)

Mix cream cheese, sugar and vanilla with electric mixer on medium speed until well blended. Add eggs; mix until blended. Remove 1 cup batter; stir in pumpkin and spices.

Pour remaining plain batter into crust. Top with pumpkin batter.

Bake at 350°F for 40 minutes or until center is almost set. Cool. Refrigerate 3 hours or overnight. Garnish with thawed COOL WHIP Whipped Topping and gumdrop cutouts (tip below).

Gumdrop Garnishes

Turn gumdrops into colorful garnishes for cheesecakes, cupcakes or other desserts. For **Gumdrop Cutouts,** roll out large gumdrops on a sugared surface. Then, cut out fancy shapes using small cookie cutters. To make a **Gumdrop Flower,** roll gumdrops flat on a lightly sugared surface. Curl up one gumdrop, then wrap a second around the outside. For leaves, cut flattened green gumdrops into stems and leaves.

PHILADELPHIA® Cream Cheese
Classic Cheesecake

Prep time: 20 minutes   Baking time: 55 minutes

Makes 12 servings

1½ **cups graham cracker crumbs**
3 **tablespoons sugar**
⅓ **cup butter *or* margarine, melted**
4 **packages (8 ounces *each*) PHILADELPHIA Cream Cheese, softened**
1 **cup sugar**
1 **teaspoon vanilla**
4 **eggs**

Mix crumbs, 3 tablespoons sugar and butter. Press onto bottom of 9-inch springform pan.

Mix cream cheese, 1 cup sugar and vanilla with electric mixer on medium speed until well blended. Add eggs; mix until blended. Pour over crust.

Bake in preheated 350°F oven for 55 minutes or until center is almost set. Loosen cake from rim of pan; cool before removing rim of pan. Refrigerate. Top with fresh fruit, if desired.

Candied Flowers

What's the secret to the stunning look of the glistening flowers on the PHILADELPHIA® Cream Cheese Classic Cheesecake shown on the cover? They're candied edible flowers, which you easily can prepare at home. Gently wash fresh edible flowers (tip, page 165) in water, then place them on white paper towels to air dry. Using a small, clean paintbrush, brush the petals with a mixture of 1 tablespoon meringue powder and 2 tablespoons water. (Look for meringue powder in specialty shops or craft stores with cake-decorating supplies.) Sprinkle the flowers with extra-fine-grain sugar, then shake off excess and let the flowers dry on wax paper for 2 to 4 hours.

If you like, you can store candied flowers in an airtight container between layers of wax paper for up to 1 week. For longer storage, freeze them for up to 6 months.

Cappuccino Cream

Prep time: 20 minutes plus refrigerating

Makes 6 servings

1   **cup freshly brewed strong MAXWELL HOUSE Coffee, at room temperature**
½   **cup milk**
1   **package (8 ounces) PHILADELPHIA Cream Cheese, softened**
1   **package (4-serving size) JELL-O Vanilla Flavor Instant Pudding & Pie Filling**
¼   **teaspoon ground cinnamon**
1   **tub (8 ounces) COOL WHIP Whipped Topping, thawed**

Beat coffee and milk gradually into cream cheese in large bowl with electric mixer on medium speed until smooth. Add pudding mix and cinnamon. Beat on low speed 1 minute. Gently stir in 2 cups of the whipped topping. Spoon mixture into 6 dessert glasses or 1-quart serving bowl.

Refrigerate until ready to serve. Just before serving, top with remaining whipped topping. Garnish with chocolate-covered coffee beans and fresh mint; sprinkle with additional ground cinnamon.

Praline Pumpkin Mousse

Prep time: 20 minutes   Refrigerating time: 4 hours

Makes 8 servings

1   **cup cold milk**
1   **can (16 ounces) pumpkin**
2   **packages (4-serving size *each*) JELL-O Vanilla Flavor Instant Pudding & Pie Filling**
1¼   **teaspoons pumpkin pie spice**
2   **cups thawed COOL WHIP Whipped Topping**
2   **tablespoons butter *or* margarine, melted**
½   **cup chopped pecans *or* walnuts**
⅓   **cup firmly packed brown sugar**

Pour milk into large bowl. Add pumpkin, pudding mixes and pumpkin pie spice. Beat with wire whisk 1 minute until well mixed. (Mixture will be thick.) Immediately stir in whipped topping. Spoon into 8 dessert glasses.

Refrigerate 4 hours or until set.

Mix butter, pecans and sugar in small bowl. Just before serving, sprinkle with pecan mixture. Garnish with additional whipped topping, ground cinnamon, fresh mint leaves and fresh currants. Store leftover mousse in refrigerator.

Speed-Soften Cream Cheese

Did you forget to take the PHILADELPHIA Cream Cheese out of the refrigerator to soften? No problem. Simply pop the unwrapped cream cheese into the microwave oven on HIGH for a few seconds until it becomes soft enough to combine easily with other ingredients. Allow 5 to 10 seconds for a 3-ounce package and 15 seconds for an 8-ounce package.

Chocolate *Berry* Dessert Cups

Prep time: 15 minutes   Refrigerating time: 2 hours

Makes 8 servings

2½   cups cold milk
2   packages (4-serving size *each*) JELL-O Chocolate Flavor Instant Pudding & Pie Filling
2   cups thawed COOL WHIP Whipped Topping
1   package (10¾ ounces) marble pound cake, cut into 1-inch cubes
2   cups raspberries *or* strawberries, hulled, halved

Pour milk into large bowl. Add pudding mixes. Beat with wire whisk 1 minute. (Mixture will be thick.) Immediately stir in whipped topping.

Spoon ⅓ of the pudding mixture into 8 dessert dishes. Top with cake cubes. Add remaining pudding mixture.

Refrigerate 2 hours or until set. Just before serving, top with raspberries. Garnish with fresh mint leaves. Store leftover dessert in refrigerator.

Berry Pointers

When choosing or picking fresh raspberries and strawberries, look for berries with healthy color for the particular variety. Once you have them home from the supermarket or berry patch, simply store them in a single layer, loosely covered, in the refrigerator until you're ready to use them. Because berries are highly perishable, they need to be used within 1 to 2 days. Just before you're ready to eat them, wash them and hull the strawberries.

Chocolate Berry
Dessert Cups
(recipe opposite page)

ONE BOWL™
Chocolate Fudge
(recipe, page 217)

Double Chocolate
Orange Nut Fudge
(recipe, page 217)

Sour Cream Pound Cake

Prep time: 25 minutes   Baking time: 1 hour and 15 minutes plus cooling

Makes 16 servings

3   **cups flour**
½   **teaspoon baking soda**
1   **cup (2 sticks) butter *or* margarine**
2¼   **cups granulated sugar**
1   **teaspoon vanilla**
6   **eggs**
1   **cup BREAKSTONE'S *or* KNUDSEN Sour Cream**
    Powdered sugar

Mix flour and baking soda in medium bowl. Beat butter in large bowl with electric mixer on medium speed until softened. Gradually add granulated sugar, beating until light and fluffy. Stir in vanilla. Add eggs, 1 at a time, mixing well after each addition. Add flour mixture alternately with sour cream, mixing well after each addition.

Spoon into greased and floured 12-cup fluted tube pan or 10-inch tube pan.

Bake at 325°F for 1 hour and 10 minutes to 1 hour and 15 minutes or until toothpick inserted in center comes out clean. Cool 10 minutes in pan on wire rack; remove from pan. Cool completely on wire rack.

Sprinkle dessert dishes with powdered sugar. Top each with a serving of cake. Garnish with fresh berries, fresh mint and fresh violets.

Double Banana *Streusel* Cake

Prep time: 15 minutes   Baking time: 55 minutes plus cooling

Makes 16 servings

1   cup POST MORNING TRADITIONS
    BANANA NUT CRUNCH Cereal
½   cup firmly packed brown sugar
1   teaspoon ground cinnamon
1   package (2-layer size) banana cake
    mix
4   eggs
1   cup BREAKSTONE'S *or* KNUDSEN Sour
    Cream
½   cup oil
    Powdered Sugar Glaze (recipe follows)

Mix cereal, sugar and cinnamon in small bowl. Beat cake mix, eggs, sour cream and oil in large bowl with electric mixer on low speed just to moisten, scraping side of bowl often. Beat on medium speed 4 minutes.

Pour ⅓ of the batter into greased and floured 12-cup fluted tube pan or 10-inch tube pan. Sprinkle with ⅓ of the cereal mixture. Repeat layers twice, ending with cereal mixture.

Bake at 350°F for 50 to 55 minutes or until cake tester inserted in center comes out clean. Cool 15 minutes in pan on wire rack; remove from pan. Cool completely on wire rack. Drizzle with Powdered Sugar Glaze. Garnish with additional cereal and walnut halves.

Powdered Sugar Glaze: Mix 1 cup sifted powdered sugar and 1 tablespoon milk in small bowl. Mix in additional milk, 1 teaspoon at a time, until glaze is smooth and of drizzling consistency.

Pastel Cupcakes

Prep time: 10 minutes   Baking time: 20 minutes plus cooling

Makes 24 cupcakes

**1   package (2-layer size) white cake mix
       or cake mix with pudding in the mix**
**¼   cup KOOL-AID Sugar-Sweetened Soft
       Drink Mix, any flavor**
**1   container (16 ounces) ready-to-spread
       vanilla frosting**

Prepare cake mix as directed on package for cupcakes, adding soft drink mix before beating. Cool completely.

Frost cooled cupcakes with frosting. Decorate with colored sprinkles, candies or gumdrop flowers (tip, page 198) or sprinkle with additional soft drink mix, if desired.

JELL-O® Ween *Poke Brownies*

Prep time: 30 minutes plus refrigerating   Baking time: 35 minutes

Makes 32

1   **package (19.8 ounces) brownie mix**
1½   **cups cold milk**
1   **package (4-serving size) JELL-O Vanilla Flavor Instant Pudding & Pie Filling Few drops *each* red and yellow food coloring**

Prepare and bake brownie mix as directed on package for 8- or 9-inch square baking pan. Remove from oven. Immediately use round handle of wooden spoon to poke holes at 1-inch intervals down through brownies to pan.

Pour cold milk into large bowl. Add pudding mix. Beat with wire whisk 2 minutes. Stir in a few drops food colorings to tint mixture orange. Quickly pour about ½ of the thin pudding evenly over warm brownies and into holes. Tap pan lightly to fill holes. Let remaining pudding mixture stand to thicken slightly. Spread remaining pudding over top of brownies to "frost." Refrigerate 1 hour or until ready to serve. Cut into 2-inch squares. Cut each square diagonally into triangles.

ONE BOWL™ *Bittersweet* Torte

Prep time: 15 minutes   Microwave time: 2 minutes   Baking time: 40 minutes

Makes 12 servings

1   package (6 squares) BAKER'S
     Bittersweet Baking Chocolate
     Squares,* divided
¾   cup (1½ sticks) butter *or* margarine
1   cup sugar
3   eggs
1   teaspoon vanilla
⅓   cup flour
¼   teaspoon salt
½   cup chopped pecans (optional)

Grease and flour 9-inch round cake pan. Line bottom of pan with wax paper.

Microwave 4 squares of the chocolate and butter in large microwavable bowl on HIGH 1½ to 2 minutes or until chocolate is almost melted, stirring halfway through heating time. Stir until chocolate is completely melted.

Stir sugar into chocolate until well blended. Mix in eggs and vanilla. Stir in flour and salt until blended. Stir in pecans. Pour into prepared pan.

Bake at 350°F for 40 minutes or until toothpick inserted in center comes out with fudgy crumbs. DO NOT OVERBAKE. Cool in pan 5 minutes. Run small knife around side of pan to loosen edge. Invert torte onto serving platter. Remove wax paper. Cool. Melt remaining 2 squares chocolate. Drizzle over top and spread on sides of torte. Garnish with chopped nuts, nuts dipped in melted chocolate, chocolate shapes (tip, page 214) and unsweetened cocoa.

*Note: Do not substitute BAKER'S Semi-Sweet Baking Chocolate Squares.

PHILADELPHIA® Cheesecake *Brownies*

Prep time: 20 minutes   Baking time: 40 minutes

Makes 24

1   **package (20½ ounces) brownie mix (do not use mixes that include a syrup pouch)**
1   **package (8 ounces) PHILADELPHIA Cream Cheese, softened**
⅓   **cup sugar**
1   **egg**
½   **teaspoon vanilla**

Prepare brownie mix as directed on package; spread in greased 13×9-inch baking pan.

Beat cream cheese with electric mixer on medium speed until smooth. Add sugar, mixing until blended. Add egg and vanilla; mix just until blended. Pour cream cheese mixture over brownie mixture; cut through with knife several times for marble effect.

Bake at 350°F for 35 to 40 minutes or until cream cheese mixture is lightly browned. Cool; cut into squares.

Chocolate Garnishes

A garnish of BAKER's Baking Chocolate can turn a simple dessert into a showy one. For **Grated Chocolate** rub a firm square of chocolate across a grater, using fine or large grates. To **Shave Chocolate,** scrape a vegetable peeler across the surface of a firm piece of chocolate. Make **Chocolate Curls** the same way except have the chocolate slightly warmer than room temperature (warm with hands). For **Chocolate Shapes** start by melting 2 squares of semi-sweet *or* bittersweet chocolate with 1 teaspoon shortening. After cooling 20 minutes, pipe onto wax paper into desired designs, such as leaves or ferns. **Chocolate Leaves** require nontoxic leaves, such as mint, lemon or strawberry leaves. With small paintbrush, spread several coats of melted chocolate on underside of each leaf. Wipe off top sides. Place leaves, chocolate-sides up, on wax paper-lined cookie sheet; refrigerate until chocolate is firm. To use, peel leaves away from chocolate. Discard leaves.

Almond *Macaroon* Brownies

Prep time: 30 minutes   Baking time: 35 minutes plus cooling

Makes 16

Brownie Layer: Microwave chocolate and butter in large microwavable bowl on HIGH 2 minutes or until butter is melted. Stir until chocolate is completely melted.

Stir ⅔ cup sugar into chocolate mixture until well blended. Add 2 eggs and vanilla; stir until completely mixed. Stir in 1 cup flour until well blended. Stir in ⅓ cup almonds.

Brownie Layer:
- **6**   **squares BAKER'S Semi-Sweet Baking Chocolate**
- **½**   **cup (1 stick) butter *or* margarine**
- **⅔**   **cup sugar**
- **2**   **eggs**
- **1**   **teaspoon vanilla**
- **1**   **cup flour**
- **⅓**   **cup chopped almonds**

Almond Macaroon Layer:
- **4**   **ounces PHILADELPHIA Cream Cheese, softened**
- **⅓**   **cup sugar**
- **1**   **egg**
- **1**   **tablespoon flour**
- **1**   **cup BAKER'S ANGEL FLAKE Coconut**
- **⅓**   **cup chopped almonds**

Line 8- or 9-inch square baking pan with foil extending over edges to form handles. Grease foil. Spread batter in prepared pan.

Almond Macaroon Layer: Mix cream cheese, ⅓ cup sugar, 1 egg and 1 tablespoon flour in same bowl until smooth. Stir in coconut and remaining ⅓ cup almonds. Spread over brownie batter.

Bake in preheated 350°F oven for 35 minutes or until toothpick inserted in center comes out with fudgy crumbs. DO NOT OVERBAKE. Cool in pan. Cut into squares.

ONE BOWL™ Chocolate *Fudge*

(Photo on page 205.)

Prep time: 15 minutes   Microwave time: 2 minutes   Refrigerating time: 2 hours

Makes 4 dozen

2 packages (8 squares *each*) BAKER'S
 Semi-Sweet Baking Chocolate Squares
1 can (14 ounces) sweetened condensed
 milk
2 teaspoons vanilla
1 cup chopped nuts *or* toasted
 BAKER'S ANGEL FLAKE Coconut

Microwave chocolate and milk in microwavable bowl on HIGH 2 minutes or until chocolate is almost melted, stirring halfway through heating time. Stir until chocolate is completely melted.

Stir in vanilla and nuts. Spread in foil-lined 8-inch square pan.

Refrigerate 2 hours or until firm. Cut into squares.

Double Chocolate Orange Nut Fudge: Prepare as directed, using 1 cup toasted chopped walnuts for nuts. Spread in pan. Before refrigerating Fudge, melt 1 package (6 squares) BAKER'S Premium White Baking Chocolate Squares as directed on package. Stir in additional ½ cup sweetened condensed milk and 1 teaspoon grated orange peel. Spread over fudge in pan.

ONE BOWL™ Citrus White
Chocolate Macaroons
(recipe, page 220) and
Shortbread Bars
(recipe opposite page)

Shortbread Bars

Prep time: 10 minutes   Baking time: 45 minutes plus cooling

Makes 2 dozen

1¼ **cups flour**
¼ **cup granulated sugar**
½ **cup (1 stick) butter *or* margarine**
1 **egg**
⅓ **cup maple-flavored syrup *or* corn syrup**
¼ **cup firmly packed brown sugar**
1 **tablespoon butter *or* margarine, melted**
1 **teaspoon vanilla**
1½ **cups POST GREAT GRAINS Cereal,
     any variety, *or* POST
     MORNING TRADITIONS
     CRANBERRY ALMOND CRUNCH Cereal**

Mix flour and granulated sugar in medium bowl. Cut in ½ cup butter until mixture resembles coarse crumbs. Press firmly onto bottom of greased 9-inch square baking pan.

Bake at 375°F for 20 minutes or until very lightly browned.

Mix egg, syrup, brown sugar, 1 tablespoon melted butter and vanilla until well blended. Stir in cereal until well coated. Spread evenly over warm crust.

Bake 20 to 25 minutes or until topping is firm around edges and slightly soft in center. Cool on wire rack. Cut into bars.

Packing Cookies

When sending cookies through the mail, prevent ending up with a box of crumbs by choosing bar cookies or other soft types. Avoid those that have frosting or pointed edges. Wrap different kinds of cookies separately. Good containers include cookie tins, rigid boxes and coffee or shortening cans. Pack the containers in a sturdy outer box with plenty of room for cushion. Pad the boxes with styrofoam pellets or plastic bubble wrap.

Coconut
Macaroons and
Chocolate-Dipped
Macaroons
(recipes opposite page)

ONE BOWL™ *Citrus*
White Chocolate Macaroons

(Photo on page 218.)

Prep time: 10 minutes   Baking time per cookie sheet: 20 minutes plus cooling

Makes 2 dozen

1	package (14 ounces) BAKER'S ANGEL FLAKE Coconut (5⅓ cups)
3	squares BAKER'S Premium White Baking Chocolate, chopped
⅔	cup sugar
6	tablespoons flour
¼	teaspoon salt
4	egg whites
2	teaspoons grated lemon, lime *or* orange peel
1	teaspoon almond extract
1	square BAKER'S Semi-Sweet Baking Chocolate, melted

Mix coconut, white chocolate, sugar, flour and salt in large bowl. Stir in egg whites, lemon peel and almond extract until well blended.

Drop by tablespoonfuls onto lightly greased and floured cookie sheets.

Bake at 325°F for 20 minutes or until edges of cookies are golden brown. Immediately remove from cookie sheets. Cool on wire racks. Drizzle with melted chocolate.

Coconut Macaroons

Prep time: 10 minutes   Baking time per cookie sheet: 20 minutes plus cooling

Makes about 3 dozen

2⅔   cups (7 ounces) BAKER'S ANGEL FLAKE
      Coconut
⅔   cup sugar
6   tablespoons flour
¼   teaspoon salt
4   egg whites
1   teaspoon almond extract
      Whole natural almonds (optional)

Mix coconut, sugar, flour and salt in large bowl. Stir in egg whites and almond extract until well blended.

Drop by teaspoonfuls onto greased and floured cookie sheets. Press 1 almond into center of each cookie.

Bake at 325°F for 20 minutes or until edges of cookies are golden brown. Immediately remove from cookie sheets. Cool on wire racks.

Chocolate-Dipped Macaroons: Prepare as directed; cool. Melt 1 package (8 squares) BAKER'S Semi-Sweet Baking Chocolate Squares as directed on package. Dip cookies halfway into chocolate; let excess chocolate drip off. Let stand at room temperature or refrigerate on wax paper-lined tray 30 minutes or until chocolate is firm.

Holiday JIGGLERS®
(recipe, page 225)

ONE BOWL™
Snowflake Brownies
(recipe opposite page)

ONE BOWL™ *Snowflake* Brownies

Prep time: 20 minutes   Microwave time: 2 minutes   Baking time: 35 minutes

Makes 12 snowflake brownies or 24 brownie squares

4   squares BAKER'S Unsweetened Baking
     Chocolate
¾   cup (1½ sticks) butter *or* margarine
2   cups sugar
3   eggs
1   teaspoon vanilla
1   cup flour

Line 13×9-inch baking pan with foil extending over edges to form handles. Grease foil.

Microwave chocolate and butter in large microwavable bowl on HIGH 2 minutes or until butter is melted. Stir until chocolate is completely melted.

Stir sugar into chocolate mixture until well blended. Mix in eggs and vanilla. Stir in flour until well blended. Spread in prepared pan.

Bake at 350°F for 30 to 35 minutes or until toothpick inserted in center comes out with fudgy crumbs. DO NOT OVERBAKE. Cool in pan. Lift out of pan onto cutting board. Cut into squares or star and round shapes using cookie cutters. Decorate cutouts to resemble snowflakes with melted BAKER'S Premium White Baking Chocolate Squares.

Quick Vanilla Rice Pudding

Prep time: 10 minutes   Cooking time: 10 minutes plus cooling

Makes 6 servings

3 **cups milk, divided**
1 **cup MINUTE White Rice, uncooked**
⅓ **cup raisins**
1 **package (4-serving size) JELL-O Vanilla Flavor Instant Pudding & Pie Filling**

Boil 1 cup of the milk. Stir in rice and raisins; cover. Let stand 5 minutes. Prepare pudding as directed on package with remaining 2 cups milk. Stir in rice mixture. Cover surface with plastic wrap; cool 5 minutes. Stir. Serve warm or chilled. Garnish with thawed COOL WHIP Whipped Topping and orange peel. Store leftover dessert in refrigerator.

Quick Vanilla
Rice Pudding
(recipe above)

Layered Chocolate
Cheesecake Triangles
(recipe opposite page)

Layered Chocolate Cheesecake Triangles

Prep time: 20 minutes   Refrigerating time: 1 hour

Makes 16 servings

1   **package (9.2 ounces)** JELL-O **No Bake Chocolate Silk Pie**
1   **package (11.1 ounces)** JELL-O **No Bake Real Cheesecake**
½   **cup (1 stick) butter *or* margarine, melted**
1⅔ **cups cold milk**
1½ **cups cold milk**

Mix Crumbs from both packages and butter thoroughly with fork in medium bowl until crumbs are well moistened. Press firmly onto bottom of foil-lined 13×9-inch pan.

Prepare Chocolate Silk Pie and Cheesecake Fillings separately with the milk, as directed on each package. Spread chocolate filling evenly over crust. Spread cheesecake filling evenly over chocolate layer.

Refrigerate at least 1 hour or until ready to serve. Garnish with drizzled melted BAKER'S Semi-Sweet Baking Chocolate. Store leftover dessert in refrigerator.

Holiday JIGGLERS®

Decorate these fun and festive JIGGLERS (photo on page 222) with colorful decorating gels or icings. Using paper towel dipped in vegetable oil, lightly wipe inside of molds. Stir 1¼ cups boiling water (do not add cold water) into 1 package (6 ounces) *or* 2 packages (3 ounces *each*) JELL-O Gelatin Dessert in a medium bowl at least 3 minutes until completely dissolved. Pour into molds to within ⅛ inch of top. Refrigerate at least 3 hours or until firm. (Gelatin does not stick to finger when touched.) Dip bottom of molds in warm water about 15 seconds. Pull gelatin away from all edges of molds with index finger. Slip finger underneath JIGGLERS and gently lift from molds. Makes 10.

Do not swallow JIGGLERS whole.

Cranberry Pear Crisp

Prep time: 15 minutes   Baking time: 30 minutes

Makes 8 servings

4 large ripe pears *or* apples, cored, peeled and sliced (4 cups)
2 tablespoons brown sugar
1 teaspoon ground cinnamon, divided
½ cup firmly packed brown sugar
½ cup flour
3 tablespoons butter *or* margarine
1 cup POST MORNING TRADITIONS CRANBERRY ALMOND CRUNCH Cereal, lightly crushed

Toss pear slices, 2 tablespoons sugar and ½ teaspoon of the cinnamon in large bowl. Spoon into 9-inch pie plate or quiche dish.

Mix ½ cup sugar, flour and remaining ½ teaspoon cinnamon in large bowl. Cut in butter until mixture resembles coarse crumbs. Stir in cereal. Sprinkle over pear slices.

Bake at 375°F for 30 minutes or until pears are tender. Garnish with pear slices and cranberries. Serve warm.

Fast Fruit Desserts

Need a quick, easy and refreshing dessert for your family? Cut up fresh or canned fruit and top with BAKER'S ANGEL FLAKE Coconut. Or, make a tasty yogurt dip for your favorite fruit by stirring 2 tablespoons KOOL-AID Sugar-Sweetened Soft Drink Mix, any flavor, with 1 container (8 ounces) vanilla low-fat yogurt *or* KNUDSEN *or* BREAKSTONE'S Sour Cream. Refrigerate 1 hour.

Sparkling *White Grape* Sorbet

Prep time: 10 minutes   Freezing time: 7½ hours

Makes 8 servings

¾ **cup boiling water**
1 **package (3 ounces) JELL-O Sparkling White Grape *or* Sparkling Wild Berry Flavor Gelatin Dessert**
½ **cup sugar**
2 **cups cold seltzer *or* champagne**

Stir boiling water into gelatin and sugar in large bowl at least 2 minutes until completely dissolved. Stir in cold seltzer. Pour into 9-inch square pan.

Freeze about 1½ hours or until ice crystals form 1 inch around edges. Spoon into blender container; cover. Blend on high speed about 30 seconds or until smooth. Return to pan.

Freeze 6 hours or overnight until firm. Scoop into dessert dishes. Garnish with edible fresh flowers (tip, page 165). Store leftover sorbet in freezer.

Note: Recipe can be frozen in ice-cream maker according to manufacturer's directions.

Impromptu Anytime

Save the day with a quick trip to your pantry or refrigerator instead of running to the store. Dinner, lunch or snacks take minutes to fix with the right ingredients on hand. Stock up on the Kraft Foods products listed on the next page plus common ingredients—such as fruits, vegetables, crackers, pizza sauce, canned tuna and pasta. Then, next time the hungries strike, just rustle up one of the quick-to-fix ideas in this chapter.

Keep-on-Hand Products

- **BAKER'S** Semi-Sweet Chocolate Chips
- **BREAKSTONE'S** or **KNUDSEN** Sour Cream
- **CHEEZ WHIZ** Process Cheese Sauce
- **COOL WHIP** Whipped Topping
- **CRACKER BARREL** Cheeses
- **GENERAL FOODS INTERNATIONAL COFFEES**
- **JELL-O** Pudding and/or Gelatin Snacks
- **KOOL-AID** Sugar-Sweetened Soft Drink Mix
- **KRAFT** Cheeses
- **KRAFT** Deluxe Macaroni & Cheese Dinner
- **KRAFT** Macaroni & Cheese Cheese Topping
- **KRAFT** Dips
- **KRAFT** Mayo Mayonnaise or **MIRACLE WHIP** Salad Dressing
- **LOUIS RICH** Oven Roasted Turkey Breast
- **OSCAR MAYER** Little Wieners or Little Smokies
- **OSCAR MAYER** Meats
- **PARM PLUS!** Seasoning Blend
- **PHILADELPHIA** Cream Cheese
- **PHILADELPHIA FLAVORS** Cream Cheese Spreads
- **POST** Cereals
- **STOVE TOP** Stuffing Mix
- **TACO BELL HOME ORIGINALS** Soft Taco Dinner Kit
- **TACO BELL HOME ORIGINALS** Thick 'N Chunky Salsa
- **TANG** Drink Mix

Anytime Snacks

■ **JELL-O Frozen Pudding and Gelatin Snacks:** Remove foil lid from JELL-O Pudding or Gelatin Snack. Insert pop stick into pudding or gelatin cup for handle. Freeze 5 hours or overnight until firm. To remove pop from cup, place bottom of cup under warm running water for 15 seconds. Press firmly on bottom of cup to release pop. (Do not twist or pull pop stick.) Once thawed, pops do not refreeze or refrigerate well.

■ **Cheesy Popcorn:** Sprinkle KRAFT Macaroni & Cheese Cheese Topping on your favorite popcorn.

■ **Cheese 'n Fruit Kabobs:** On short metal or wooden skewers, thread cubes of KRAFT Cheese and pieces of assorted fresh fruit, such as grapes, strawberries, pineapple, apple or banana. Serve with strawberry preserves or grape jelly for dipping, if desired.

■ **Bite-Size Snacks:** Heat OSCAR MAYER Little Wieners or Little Smokies in a prepared sauce, such as bottled barbecue sauce, canned cheese soup or hot mustard.

■ **Cream Cheese Bites:** Spread PHILADELPHIA FLAVORS Strawberry Cream Cheese Spread on graham crackers or cookies. Top with cut-up fresh fruit and chocolate chips.

■ **Cheese and Crackers:** Top crackers with sliced CRACKER BARREL Cheese and fruit or jelly.

■ **Vegetable Bites:** Spoon KRAFT Dip into hollowed-out thick zucchini slices, cherry tomatoes or steamed small red potatoes.

■ **Bumps on a Log:** Spread PHILADELPHIA FLAVORS Apple Cinnamon Cream Cheese onto celery sticks; top with raisins or peanuts.

■ **Tortilla Swirls:** Spread PHILADELPHIA Cream Cheese or CHEEZ WHIZ Process Cheese Sauce onto a tortilla. Top with lettuce and OSCAR MAYER Sliced Meats. Roll up.

Main Dishes

■ **Personalized Pizza:** Set out readymade pizza crust, pizza sauce and a variety of toppings, including OSCAR MAYER Meats and KRAFT Cheeses, so folks can create their own combinations. Bake as directed on crust package.

■ **Pepperoni Macaroni:** Start with KRAFT Deluxe Macaroni & Cheese Dinner and stir in chopped pepperoni and a pinch of oregano and garlic.

■ **Baked Bean Fix-Up:** Add OSCAR MAYER Little Wieners or Little Smokies to baked beans for added flavor and protein.

■ **Leftover Magic:** Top slices of meat with a sauce made from canned soup and a pinch of herb. Serve with prepared STOVE TOP Stuffing Mix.

■ **Stir-Fry Sensation:** Stir-fry vegetables and strips of LOUIS RICH Oven Roasted Turkey Breast in a little oil. Stir in stir-fry sauce and serve over hot MINUTE White Rice.

■ **Easy Cheesy Taco Melts:** Using the TACO BELL HOME ORIGINALS Soft Taco Dinner Kit, prepare meat as directed. Place 1 KRAFT Singles Process Cheese Food slice on Tortilla. Top with meat and Taco Sauce. Roll up. Microwave on HIGH 15 to 30 seconds or until process cheese food is melted. Top with desired toppings, such as KRAFT Shredded Cheese, BREAKSTONE'S or KNUDSEN Sour Cream and TACO BELL HOME ORIGINALS Thick 'N Chunky Salsa.

■ **Tuna Macaroni Deluxe:** Add a can of drained and flaked tuna and thawed frozen peas with the cheese when preparing KRAFT Deluxe Macaroni & Cheese Dinner.

TACO BELL and HOME ORIGINALS are registered trademarks owned and licensed by Taco Bell Corp.

232

Side Dishes

■ **Potato Topping:** Spoon KRAFT Dip onto a baked potato.

■ **Stuffing on the Side:** Stir chopped apple, nuts and raisins into prepared STOVE TOP Stuffing Mix.

■ **Spruce Up Side Dishes:** Sprinkle PARM PLUS! Seasoning Blend on pasta, rice or casseroles, or stir it into soups, dips or salad dressings.

■ **Spark Up Salads:** Use tomato juice or spicy seasoned tomato juice instead of water when preparing GOOD SEASONS Honey French Salad Dressing Mix. Or, for a fruity fat free dressing, substitute orange, cranberry or grapefruit juice for the water when making GOOD SEASONS Fat Free Italian Salad Dressing Mix.

■ **Handy Salads:** Turn to KRAFT Mayo Real Mayonnaise or MIRACLE WHIP Salad Dressing to flavor packages of coleslaw mix, tossed with cumin or celery seeds. Or, mix chopped red and green apples with KRAFT Mayo Real Mayonnaise or MIRACLE WHIP Salad Dressing, adding raisins, chopped walnuts and sliced celery.

Desserts and Beverages

■ **Bubbly Beverage:** Place 2 tablespoons KOOL-AID Sugar-Sweetened Soft Drink Mix in a tall glass. Slowly stir in 1 cup cold club soda or seltzer. Add ice cubes; serve immediately.

■ **Crunchy Parfait:** Alternate layers of fruit-flavored yogurt, sliced fresh fruit or berries and your favorite variety of crunchy POST Cereal.

■ **Tapioca Mix-Ins:** Start with JELL-O Tapioca Pudding Snacks and mix-in one of the following: 1 tablespoon raisins or GENERAL FOODS INTERNATIONAL COFFEES, Suisse Mocha Flavor; 1/8 teaspoon ground cinnamon; 2 teaspoons BAKER'S Semi-Sweet Real Chocolate Chips; or some thawed COOL WHIP Whipped Topping.

■ **Dessert in a Glass:** Mix prepared TANG Drink Mix with softened vanilla ice cream. Or, pour prepared TANG Drink Mix, KOOl-AID Soft Drink Mix or iced tea over scoops of fruit sherbet or sorbet.

T-Z

Tips

METRIC COOKING HINTS

By making a few conversions, cooks in Australia, Canada and the United Kingdom can use the recipes in this book with confidence. The charts on this page provide a guide for converting measurements from the U.S. customary system, which is used throughout this book, to the imperial and metric systems. There also is a conversion table for oven temperatures to accommodate the differences in oven calibrations.

Product Differences: Most of the ingredients called for in the recipes in this book are available in English-speaking countries. However, some are known by different names. Here are some common American ingredients and their possible counterparts:
■ Sugar is granulated or castor sugar.
■ Powdered sugar is icing sugar.
■ All-purpose flour is plain household flour or white flour. When self-rising flour is used in place of all-purpose flour in a recipe that calls for leavening, omit the leavening agent (baking soda or baking powder) and salt.
■ Light-colored corn syrup is golden syrup.
■ Cornstarch is cornflour.
■ Baking soda is bicarbonate of soda.
■ Vanilla is vanilla essence.
■ Green, red or yellow sweet peppers are capsicums.
■ Golden raisins are sultanas.

Volume and Weight: Americans traditionally use cup measures for liquid and solid ingredients. The chart, below, shows the approximate imperial and metric equivalents. If you are accustomed to weighing solid ingredients, the following approximate equivalents will be helpful.
■ 1 cup butter, castor sugar or rice = 8 ounces = about 250 grams
■ 1 cup flour = 4 ounces = about 125 grams
■ 1 cup icing sugar = 5 ounces = about 150 grams
    Spoon measures are used for smaller amounts of ingredients. Although the size of the tablespoon varies slightly in different countries, for practical purposes and for recipes in this book, a straight substitution is all that's necessary.
    Measurements made using cups or spoons always should be level unless stated otherwise.

EQUIVALENTS: U.S. = AUSTRALIA/U.K.

⅛ teaspoon = 0.5 ml
¼ teaspoon = 1 ml
½ teaspoon = 2 ml
1 teaspoon = 5 ml
1 tablespoon = 1 tablespoon
¼ cup = 2 tablespoons = 2 fluid ounces = 60 ml
⅓ cup = ¼ cup = 3 fluid ounces = 90 ml
½ cup = ⅓ cup = 4 fluid ounces = 120 ml
⅔ cup = ½ cup = 5 fluid ounces = 150 ml
¾ cup = ⅔ cup = 6 fluid ounces = 180 ml
1 cup = ¾ cup = 8 fluid ounces = 240 ml
1¼ cups = 1 cup
2 cups = 1 pint
1 quart = 1 litre
½ inch = 1.27 cm
1 inch = 2.54 cm

BAKING PAN SIZES

American	Metric
8×1½-inch round baking pan	20×4-centimetre cake tin
9×1½-inch round baking pan	23×3.5-centimetre cake tin
11×7×1½-inch baking pan	28×18×4-centimetre baking tin
13×9×2-inch baking pan	30×20×3-centimetre baking tin
2-quart rectangular baking dish	30×20×3-centimetre baking tin
15×10×1-inch baking pan	30×25×2-centimetre baking tin (Swiss roll tin)
9-inch pie plate	22×4- or 23×4-centimetre pie plate
7- or 8-inch springform pan	18- or 20-centimetre springform or loose-bottom cake tin
9×5×3-inch loaf pan	23×13×7-centimetre or 2-pound narrow loaf tin or pâté tin
1½-quart casserole	1.5-litre casserole
2-quart casserole	2-litre casserole

OVEN TEMPERATURE EQUIVALENTS

Fahrenheit Setting	Celsius Setting*	Gas Setting
300°F	150°C	Gas Mark 2 (slow)
325°F	160°C	Gas Mark 3 (moderately slow)
350°F	180°C	Gas Mark 4 (moderate)
375°F	190°C	Gas Mark 5 (moderately hot)
400°F	200°C	Gas Mark 6 (hot)
425°F	220°C	Gas Mark 7
450°F	230°C	Gas Mark 8 (very hot)
Broil		Grill

* Electric and gas ovens may be calibrated using Celsius. However, for an electric oven, increase the Celsius setting 10 to 20 degrees when cooking above 160°C. For convection or forced-air ovens (gas or electric), lower the temperature setting 10°C when cooking at all heat levels.